THE ENCYCLOPEDIA OF PSYCHOACTIVE DRUGS

SERIES 1

The Addictive Personality
Alcohol and Alcoholism
Alcohol Customs and Rituals
Alcohol Teenage Drinking
Amphetamines Danger in the Fast Lane
Barbiturates Sleeping Potion or Intoxicant?
Caffeine The Most Popular Stimulant
Cocaine A New Epidemic
Escape from Anxiety and Stress
Flowering Plants Magic in Bloom
Getting Help Treatments for Drug Abuse
Heroin The Street Narcotic
Inhalants The Toxic Fumes

LSD Visions or Nightmares?
Marijuana Its Effects on Mind & Body
Methadone Treatment for Addiction
Mushrooms Psychedelic Fungi
Nicotine An Old-Fashioned Addiction
Over-The-Counter Drugs Harmless or Hazardous?
PCP The Dangerous Angel
Prescription Narcotics The Addictive Painkillers
Quaaludes The Quest for Oblivion
Teenage Depression and Drugs
Treating Mental Illness
Valium and Other Tranquilizers

SERIES 2

Bad Trips
Brain Function
Case Histories
Celebrity Drug Use
Designer Drugs
The Downside of Drugs
Drinking, Driving, and Drugs
Drugs and Civilization
Drugs and Crime
Drugs and Diet
Drugs and Disease
Drugs and Emotion
Drugs and Pain
Drugs and Perception
Drugs and Pregnancy
Drugs and Sexual Behavior

Drugs and Sleep
Drugs and Sports
Drugs and the Arts
Drugs and the Brain
Drugs and the Family
Drugs and the Law
Drugs and Women
Drugs of the Future
Drugs Through the Ages
Drug Use Around the World
Legalization A Debate
Mental Disturbances
Nutrition and the Brain
The Origins and Sources of Drugs
Substance Abuse Prevention and Cures
Who Uses Drugs?

LEGALIZATION: A DEBATE

GENERAL EDITOR
Professor Solomon H. Snyder, M.D.

*Distinguished Service Professor of
Neuroscience, Pharmacology, and Psychiatry at
The Johns Hopkins University School of Medicine*

•

ASSOCIATE EDITOR
Professor Barry L. Jacobs, Ph.D.

*Program in Neuroscience, Department of Psychology,
Princeton University*

•

SENIOR EDITORIAL CONSULTANT
Joann Rodgers

*Deputy Director, Office of Public Affairs at
The Johns Hopkins Medical Institutions*

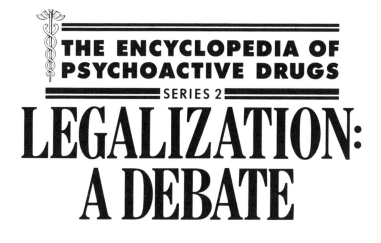

THE ENCYCLOPEDIA OF PSYCHOACTIVE DRUGS

SERIES 2

LEGALIZATION: A DEBATE

ELIOT MARSHALL

CHELSEA HOUSE PUBLISHERS

NEW YORK • NEW HAVEN • PHILADELPHIA

EDITOR-IN-CHIEF: Nancy Toff
EXECUTIVE EDITOR: Remmel T. Nunn
MANAGING EDITOR: Karyn Gullen Browne
COPY CHIEF: Juliann Barbato
PICTURE EDITOR: Adrian G. Allen
ART DIRECTOR: Giannella Garrett
MANUFACTURING MANAGER: Gerald Levine

Staff for LEGALIZATION: A DEBATE

SENIOR EDITOR: Jane Larkin Crain
ASSOCIATE EDITOR: Paula Edelson
ASSISTANT EDITOR: Laura-Ann Dolce
COPY EDITOR: Michael Goodman
EDITORIAL ASSISTANT: Susan DeRosa
ASSOCIATE PICTURE EDITOR: Juliette Dickstein
PICTURE RESEARCHER: Villette Harris
DESIGNER: Victoria Tomaselli
PRODUCTION COORDINATOR: Joseph Romano
COVER ILLUSTRATION: Hrana L. Janto

CREATIVE DIRECTOR: Harold Steinberg

3 5 7 9 8 6 4 2
Library of Congress Cataloging in Publication Data

Marshall, Eliot.
    Legalization: a debate / Eliot Marshall.
    p.   cm.—(The Encyclopedia of psychoactive drugs.
    Series 2)
    Bibliography: p.
    Includes index.
    1. Drugs—Law and legislation—United States—Juvenile
literature. 2. Marihuana—Law and legislation—United
States—Juvenile literature. 3. Drugs—Law and legislation—
Juvenile literature. 4. Marihuana—Law and legislation—
Juvenile literature. [1. Drugs—Law and legislation.] I. Title.
II. Series.
KF3885.Z9M37   1988   344.73'0545—dc19
[347.304545]   87–23271

ISBN 1-55546-229-4

CONTENTS

Congress, which meets in the Capitol in Washington, D.C., is responsible for enacting U.S. laws. Because Congress is elected by the American people, the legislation it passes reflects public attitudes.

FOREWORD

In the Mainstream
of American Life

One of the legacies of the social upheaval of the 1960s is that psychoactive drugs have become part of the mainstream of American life. Schools, homes, and communities cannot be "drug proofed." There is a demand for drugs — and the supply is plentiful. Social norms have changed and drugs are not only available—they are everywhere.

But where efforts to curtail the supply of drugs and outlaw their use have had tragically limited effects on demand, it may be that education has begun to stem the rising tide of drug abuse among young people and adults alike.

Over the past 25 years, as drugs have become an increasingly routine facet of contemporary life, a great many teenagers have adopted the notion that drug taking was somehow a right or a privilege or a necessity. They have done so, however, without understanding the consequences of drug use during the crucial years of adolescence.

The teenage years are few in the total life cycle, but critical in the maturation process. During these years adolescents face the difficult tasks of discovering their identity, clarifying their sexual roles, asserting their independence, learning to cope with authority, and searching for goals that will give their lives meaning.

Drugs rob adolescents of precious time, stamina, and health. They interrupt critical learning processes, sometimes forever. Teenagers who use drugs are likely to withdraw increasingly into themselves, to "cop out" at just the time when they most need to reach out and experience the world.

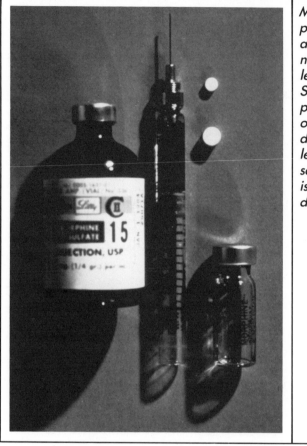

Morphine, an effective pain reliever that is also a highly addictive narcotic, is used legally in the United States for medical purposes. Whether other psychoactive drugs should be legalized under the same conditions is an issue that is still under debate.

Fortunately, as a recent Gallup poll shows, young people are beginning to realize this, too. They themselves label drugs their most important problem. In the last few years, moreover, the climate of tolerance and ignorance surrounding drugs has been changing.

Adolescents as well as adults are becoming aware of mounting evidence that every race, ethnic group, and class is vulnerable to drug dependency.

Recent publicity about the cost and failure of drug rehabilitation efforts; dangerous drug use among pilots, air traffic controllers, star athletes, and Hollywood celebrities; and drug-related accidents, suicides, and violent crime have focused the public's attention on the need to wage an all-out war on drug abuse before it seriously undermines the fabric of society itself.

The anti-drug message is getting stronger and there is evidence that the message is beginning to get through to adults and teenagers alike.

The Encyclopedia of Psychoactive Drugs hopes to play a part in the national campaign now underway to educate young people about drugs. Series 1 provides clear and comprehensive discussions of common psychoactive substances, outlines their psychological and physiological effects on the mind and body, explains how they "hook" the user, and separates fact from myth in the complex issue of drug abuse.

Whereas Series 1 focuses on specific drugs, such as nicotine or cocaine, Series 2 confronts a broad range of both social and physiological phenomena. Each volume addresses the ramifications of drug use and abuse on some aspect of human experience: social, familial, cultural, historical, and physical. Separate volumes explore questions about the effects of drugs on brain chemistry and unborn children; the use and abuse of painkillers; the relationship between drugs and sexual behavior, sports, and the arts; drugs and disease; the role of drugs in history; and the sophisticated drugs now being developed in the laboratory that will profoundly change the future.

Each book in the series is fully illustrated and is tailored to the needs and interests of young readers. The more adolescents know about drugs and their role in society, the less likely they are to misuse them.

Joann Rodgers
Senior Editorial Consultant

A pharmacist prepares marijuana tablets for use in research. The same drugs that can cure disease and relieve pain when taken under careful supervision can cause severe illness and even death if abused.

INTRODUCTION

The Gift of Wizardry
Use and Abuse

JACK H. MENDELSON, M.D.
NANCY K. MELLO, Ph.D.
Alcohol and Drug Abuse Research Center
Harvard Medical School—McLean Hospital

Dorothy to the Wizard:

"I think you are a very bad man," said Dorothy.
"Oh no, my dear; I'm really a very good man; but I'm a very bad Wizard."
—from THE WIZARD OF OZ

Man is endowed with the gift of wizardry, a talent for discovery and invention. The discovery and invention of substances that change the way we feel and behave are among man's special accomplishments, and, like so many other products of our wizardry, these substances have the capacity to harm as well as to help. Psychoactive drugs can cause profound changes in the chemistry of the brain and other vital organs, and although their legitimate use can relieve pain and cure disease, their abuse leads in a tragic number of cases to destruction.

Consider alcohol — available to all and yet regarded with intense ambivalence from biblical times to the present day. The use of alcoholic beverages dates back to our earliest ancestors. Alcohol use and misuse became associated with the worship of gods and demons. One of the most powerful Greek gods was Dionysus, lord of fruitfulness and god of wine. The Romans adopted Dionysus but changed his name to Bacchus. Festivals and holidays associated with Bacchus celebrated the harvest and the origins of life. Time has blurred the images of the Bacchanalian festival, but the theme of drunkenness as a major part of celebration has survived the pagan gods and remains a familiar part of modern society. The term "Bacchanalian Festival" conveys a more appealing image than "drunken orgy" or "pot party," but whatever the label, drinking alcohol is a form of drug use that results in addiction for millions.

The fact that many millions of other people can use alcohol in moderation does not mitigate the toll this drug takes on society as a whole. According to reliable estimates, one out of every ten Americans develops a serious alcohol-related problem sometime in his or her lifetime. In addition, automobile accidents caused by drunken drivers claim the lives of tens of thousands every year. Many of the victims are gifted young people, just starting out in adult life. Hospital emergency rooms abound with patients seeking help for alcohol-related injuries.

Who is to blame? Can we blame the many manufacturers who produce such an amazing variety of alcoholic beverages? Should we blame the educators who fail to explain the perils of intoxication, or so exaggerate the dangers of drinking that no one could possibly believe them? Are friends to blame — those peers who urge others to "drink more and faster," or the macho types who stress the importance of being able to "hold your liquor"? Casting blame, however, is hardly constructive, and pointing the finger is a fruitless way to deal with the problem. Alcoholism and drug abuse have few culprits but many victims. Accountability begins with each of us, every time we choose to use or misuse an intoxicating substance.

It is ironic that some of man's earliest medicines, derived from natural plant products, are used today to poison and to intoxicate. Relief from pain and suffering is one of society's many continuing goals. Over 3,000 years ago, the Therapeutic Papyrus of Thebes, one of our earliest written records, gave instructions for the use of opium in the treatment of pain. Opium, in the form of its major derivative, morphine, and similar compounds, such as heroin, have also been used by many to induce changes in mood and feeling. Another example of man's misuse of a natural substance is the coca leaf, which for centuries was used by the Indians of Peru to reduce fatigue and hunger. Its modern derivative, cocaine, has important medical use as a local anesthetic. Unfortunately, its increasing abuse in the 1980s clearly has reached epidemic proportions.

The purpose of this series is to explore in depth the psychological and behavioral effects that psychoactive drugs have on the individual, and also, to investigate the ways in which drug use influences the legal, economic, cultural, and even moral aspects of societies. The information presented here (and in other books in this series) is based on many clinical and laboratory studies and other observations by people from diverse walks of life.

Over the centuries, novelists, poets, and dramatists have provided us with many insights into the sometimes seductive but ultimately problematic aspects of alcohol and drug use. Physicians, lawyers, biologists, psychologists, and social scientists have contributed to a better understanding of the causes and consequences of using these substances. The authors in this series have attempted to gather and condense all the latest information about drug use and abuse. They have also described the sometimes wide gaps in our knowledge and have suggested some new ways to answer many difficult questions.

One such question, for example, is how do alcohol and drug problems get started? And what is the best way to treat them when they do? Not too many years ago, alcoholics and drug abusers were regarded as evil, immoral, or both. It is now recognized that these persons suffer from very complicated diseases involving deep psychological and social problems. To understand how the disease begins and progresses, it is necessary to understand the nature of the substance, the behavior of addicts, and the characteristics of the society or culture in which they live.

Although many of the social environments we live in are very similar, some of the most subtle differences can strongly influence our thinking and behavior. Where we live, go to school and work, whom we discuss things with — all influence our opinions about drug use and misuse. Yet we also share certain commonly accepted beliefs that outweigh any differences in our attitudes. The authors in this series have tried to identify and discuss the central, most crucial issues concerning drug use and misuse.

Despite the increasing sophistication of the chemical substances we create in the laboratory, we have a long way to go in our efforts to make these powerful drugs work for us rather than against us.

The volumes in this series address a wide range of timely questions. What influence has drug use had on the arts? Why do so many of today's celebrities and star athletes use drugs, and what is being done to solve this problem? What is the relationship between drugs and crime? What is the physiological basis for the power drugs can hold over us? These are but a few of the issues explored in this far-ranging series.

Educating people about the dangers of drugs can go a long way towards minimizing the desperate consequences of substance abuse for individuals and society as a whole. Luckily, human beings have the resources to solve even the most serious problems that beset them, once they make the commitment to do so. As one keen and sensitive observer, Dr. Lewis Thomas, has said,

> There is nothing at all absurd about the human condition. We matter. It seems to me a good guess, hazarded by a good many people who have thought about it, that we may be engaged in the formation of something like a mind for the life of this planet. If this is so, we are still at the most primitive stage, still fumbling with language and thinking, but infinitely capacitated for the future. Looked at this way, it is remarkable that we've come as far as we have in so short a period, really no time at all as geologists measure time. We are the newest, youngest, and the brightest thing around.

LEGALIZATION:
A DEBATE

This carving of Blind Justice graces the Brooklyn State Courthouse. One must weigh both sides of the issue before forming an opinion as to whether certain drugs that are now illicit should be legal.

EDITOR'S PREFACE

This volume introduces the reader to the legal issues surrounding the use and abuse of psychoactive drugs. It then focuses on the controversy over whether or not currently illicit substances should be legalized. Arguing for legalization, a number of medical researchers and users alike have asked in recent years, "Why not make marijuana legal, like alcohol?" Some physicians who daily witness the final agonies of terminal cancer patients advocate the limited legalization of heroin for use in the alleviation of this suffering. For their part, civil libertarians argue that antidrug laws violate constitutional rights to privacy.

On the other side of this debate is a network of law enforcement officials, health care professionals, and informed laymen who adamantly oppose any move to loosen current prohibitions against mind-altering drugs. Such people maintain that making drugs more accessible in any way will only exacerbate the epidemic of abuse and addiction. Further, they hold that society has the legal right to protect its members against the kinds of physical and mental illnesses that psychoactive drugs can precipitate.

Legalization: A Debate gives voice to these opposing views. The editors would like to emphasize that we are not taking sides in this debate. However, we would also like to make it clear that when it comes to drug *use*, there really can be no debate. The 52-volume Encyclopedia of Psychoactive Drugs amply documents the array of negative side effects that potentially attends even casual experimentation with any drug, from nicotine and alcohol to marijuana, cocaine, and heroin. This volume in no way endorses the use of illicit drugs.

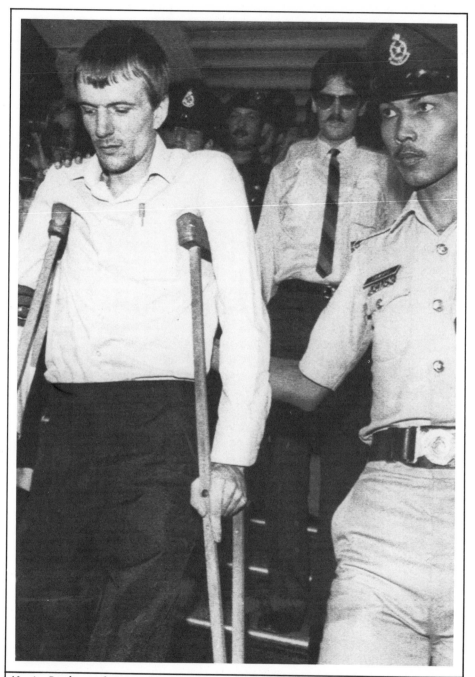

Kevin Barlow of Australia leaves a Malaysian court after being sentenced to death for drug trafficking. Foreigners who break a country's laws often receive the same penalties as native criminals.

AUTHOR'S PREFACE

That eyesore — " said Shan-Fook, nodding toward a squat old building encircled by barbed wire on the right side of the car. "It shouldn't be there." We were driving in heavy traffic toward the sleek new office towers in downtown Kuala Lumpur, a large city in Malaysia.

"What is it?" I asked.

"That's our hanging prison," he said. "If you get caught with drugs, that's where they hang you."

Shan-Fook, who edits a local paper, explained that Malaysia had been embarrassed many years earlier when a drug ring broken up in Europe revealed that it had obtained its supplies from Malaysian runners. Back home, the government declared it would end the drug trade. Its tool was fear. The majority of Malaysians are Muslim, and the Koran, the sacred text of the Islamic religion, forbids intoxicants. Thus, there was little opposition to a harsh new law mandating the death penalty for anyone found with 15 grams or more of heroin. There are other harsh penalties for possession of any of a long list of drugs, including marijuana. Signs warn all travelers as they enter the country that Malaysia imposes the death penalty on traffickers.

I had read the signs, but assumed they would not apply to someone from a tolerant Western country, like my own United States. I was wrong. Shan-Fook said that two young Australian men and a young French woman had recently been sentenced to hang. Because of an international appeal on her behalf, the woman's sentence had been reduced to life in prison. The men — Kevin Barlow and Brian Chambers — were hanged shortly after my visit, at 6 o'clock one June morning in 1986. Their bodies were carried out to their bereaved parents, who stood outside the building I had seen on my way to town.

The Malaysian government exhibited this model of the gallows used to hang drug traffickers, hoping to discourage would-be criminals.

That is Malaysia's tough approach to drug peddling. Not far away, in Nepal, deep in the Himalayan mountains, one finds a different scene. In Nepal, drug use is an accepted part of life. The government does not enforce standards of behavior, and in fact collects taxes on the drug trade. Not only are drugs tolerated, but marijuana and hashish are sold openly in shops licensed by the state.

This policy has several damaging effects, such as the suffering of those who become addicted because drugs are so freely available. But it also has its advantages. There is, for example, no need to support a large drug police force; no burden on the judicial system to sort out the major from the minor offenders; no need to house and feed drug criminals in jail; no agony for the families of those caught in the coils of the law; and no special incentive for traffickers to hide their business from the tax collector.

These extreme attitudes — Malaysian stringency and Nepalese leniency — are both represented in America's approach to the problem of drug abuse. The abuse of psychoactive substances has been labeled a national crisis during some periods but virtually ignored during others. Likewise, American attitudes on the issues of punishment and legalization have changed from decade to decade. This volume attempts to pull together information from both sides of the debate. Some of it is history, some medicine and science, and some philosophy.

The book, which follows the format of a trial, is divided into two sections. After an opening statement, it presents evidence both for and against legalization. This part is supposed to be free of speculation and hearsay and will present "just the facts." The jury in the case is the reader, who should weigh evidence on both sides in deciding whether certain drugs that are now illicit should be made legal.

The factual presentation makes up the first four chapters and deals with the history of drug laws, their rationale, some exceptions, and medical uses of drugs. Some dangers of drug use are discussed, as are the expert guesses about patterns of abuse. There is also a section on alcohol and its prohibition. The historical record on alcohol may teach some interesting lessons about drug prohibition in general. Once the evidence is on the table, as in any trial, the argument begins. This takes place in the last chapters: "For Legalization" and "For Prohibition." The drug considered is marijuana because of its pervasive use and because it is the most likely candidate for a real legalization campaign. In this trial, both sides are represented by the same advocate, who has no strong bias and hopes to give fair representation to both positions. If this method works as intended, readers will find the case that makes the most sense to them, based on their beliefs and experiences. They should also be able to learn something new from the other side, one of the advantages that makes debating worthwhile.

A New York City opium den in 1883. Unlike tobacco and alcohol, opium never entered the American mainstream, and its recreational use has always taken place behind closed doors.

CHAPTER 1

70 YEARS OF DRUG PROHIBITION

Until early in the 20th century, such addictive drugs as opium and morphine were used freely in the United States. Doctors prescribed them to treat a wide variety of ailments, but it was not even necessary to go to a doctor to get a "fix." In many states, elixirs spiked with potent chemicals were available in drugstores; there was also no federal law against selling narcotics.

A survey in the state of Iowa in the 1880s found that 3,000 grocery stores sold opiates without a prescription. Hard drugs were available in many patent medicines such as McMunn's Elixir of Opium, Ayer's Cherry Pectoral, and Mrs. Winslow's Soothing Syrup, which were advertised as remedies for almost any problem, from father's upset stomach to baby's sore gums. Even the soft drink Coca-Cola contained cocaine until 1903, when the recipe was changed and caffeine was substituted.

This rather free and tolerant attitude toward drugs, which was based largely on ignorance, was challenged in the early 1900s by the journalist Samuel Hopkins Adams. From 1905 to 1907 Adams published in *Collier's* magazine a series entitled "The Great American Fraud," which described the hidden menace of patent medicines. Such literature, along with pressure from activists who argued that innocent people were becoming addicted because they did not know their medicines were loaded with potentially dangerous and addictive drugs, led to the passage in 1906 of the Pure Food and Drug Act.

This law required that manufacturers of patent medicines list ingredients on the label. One estimate (possibly exaggerated) is that this labeling change reduced the sale of drugged medicines by one-third. In any case, the law appears to have had little impact on the volume of narcotics imported into the United States, which continued to rise. The law did, however, lay the groundwork for other attempts to control the use of psychoactive substances.

The Harrison Act

In 1914, Congress passed another narcotics-control law, called the Harrison Act. The motives for passing this bill were not only moral but economic as well. In the early 1900s the State Department of the United States was interested in im-

A late-19th-century advertisement for Mrs. Winslow's Syrup, a medication that contained opium. Until 1906, when the sale of drugs was limited by law, opiates such as heroin were sold over the counter.

The journalist Samuel Hopkins Adams used the media to warn against patent medicines. Increased awareness about the dangers of addiction led to the passage of the first antidrug laws in the early 20th century.

proving relations with China. It hoped that better relations would bring better opportunities for U.S. merchants who wanted to expand trade in the Orient. Chinese administrators were deeply engaged in a battle against opium smoking, a problem in the cities. The opium business in China was dominated by European importers, and American leaders realized that they might be able to win favor in China (at no great cost to traders) by joining an international drug control program. Many U.S. leaders were also motivated by feelings of moral outrage.

To participate in the international program, nations had to control drug use at home. But the United States had no federal drug laws. Spurred by its trade ambitions, the government rapidly became an advocate of narcotics control. The Wilson administration originally wanted harsher law than the one passed by Congress several years later. The early bill would have imposed direct controls on opiates and cocaine. The law that actually passed in 1914 required only the registering and monitoring of certain drug sales. Doctors and patent medicine companies had lobbied to undo some strict sections of the original scheme, with some success.

Under the Harrison Act, patent medicines were allowed to contain opiates and cocaine — but only a regulated amount, and only if correctly labeled. Doctors were now allowed to dispense drugs only in person. They were also required to keep extensive records. All wholesale buyers (pharmacies, manufacturers, doctors) were required to register and keep track of purchases. A massive record-keeping apparatus went into effect.

Because the Harrison Act regulated rather than prohibited the use of morphine and cocaine, some of its clauses were open to different interpretations. For example, one clause stated that doctors were allowed to give narcotics "prescribed in good faith." Some interpreters took this to mean that drugs could be used only for medicinal purposes, such as relieving pain caused by illness or injury. But others thought that it meant that doctors could prescribe these drugs in moderate doses for addicts going through the agonies of sudden withdrawal. These different interpretations of the law sparked a controversy that continues to this day.

The Meaning of Addiction

At the heart of the quarrel was a battle between doctors and the strict interpreters of the Harrison Act over the meaning of "addiction." In the early years, many doctors argued — and no doubt sincerely believed — that an addict could die if denied the drug he or she needed. This was based on a theory that drugs changed a person's immune system, making an addict dependent on the drug to remain capable of fighting off disease. Drug withdrawal therefore was thought to make a person vulnerable to a breakdown of the immune system. This theory proved wrong. But even now, relatively little is known about why an addict's individual chemistry and psychology are different from a nonaddict's. It is clear that some people are more likely to get "hooked" than others. Yet there is no reliable way of unhooking a person, once addicted.

Medical professionals argued that they were more likely to get to the bottom of this problem than law enforcement officials were. They took a scientific approach, one that tried to avoid moralizing and focused on how drug abuse works. Doctors tended to be more tolerant of addicts, regarding them as victims of a disease. In this way, many doctors said that providing drugs to an addict was not evil but rather an effort to help them control a physical problem. Many people were suspicious of this opinion, for they pointed out that some doctors had a financial stake in narcotics sales: They made a living by treating addicts.

At the other extreme of opinion was the strict enforcement approach. Those who took this view tended to see addicts as morally weak. They believed that drug abuse resulted from a lack of self-control. In the early 1900s many people thought that society would be giving in to the same kind of weakness shown by the addict if it tolerated addiction. The best approach, in this view, was to outlaw nonmedical use of drugs and to define "medical use" very narrowly. Every suspect use of drugs, they said, ought to be banned. If the addict was too weak to help him- or herself, society would provide the self-discipline. By outlawing addictive drugs and making them hard to get, the enforcers hoped to reduce the number of addicts.

Tightening the Controls

Another argument involving the Harrison Act concerned the way the law should be enforced. At first, the federal government was divided on this issue. The Public Health Service, staffed by physicians, leaned toward the view that the Harrison Act merely required elaborate record keeping and did not call for a federal drug police force. The Bureau of Internal Revenue (predecessor to the Internal Revenue Service), empowered to enforce the Act, claimed it was authorized to arrest people. A test of the law came early.

In 1916 the case of *U.S. v. Jin Fuey Moy,* which involved an arrest for drug possession made by federal agents, came before the Supreme Court. Did the Harrison Act permit Internal Revenue agents to arrest someone simply for possessing narcotics, as the agents claimed? Or was enforcement to

Supreme Court Justice Oliver Wendell Holmes's liberal reading of the Harrison Act sparked a campaign for stronger enforcement of antidrug laws.

be left to the individual states? The Supreme Court, led by Justice Oliver Wendell Holmes, decided the federal agents were wrong: Congress had not granted power to the Bureau of Internal Revenue to prevent narcotic use. It had granted power only to collect information and taxes.

The Supreme Court decision was a challenge to the advocates of stronger enforcement. They mobilized a committee of inquiry that gathered information on narcotics abuse and presented it to Congress as an argument for stronger controls. In the two decades that followed, many changes were made in the law, and by the 1940s the narcotics enforcement agents had the authority they sought. Important steps on the way to modern drug enforcement policy were as follows:

In 1919 Congress passed a law that empowered Internal Revenue agents to intervene between the doctor and the patient and to enforce the view that the regular use of drugs, even in a medical context, could be prohibited. Abusers were subject to Federal prosecution. These new powers were solidified by a narrow (5–4) Supreme Court decision the same year, which ruled that giving narcotics to support an addict's habit was not a valid medical use of drugs.

Between 1919 and 1925 the federal government and New York State moved to close down a number of addict-maintenance clinics. Concerned doctors had started the clinics as a haven for addicts who found themselves the target of a new law-enforcement campaign. Because the clinics "treated" patients by giving them narcotics, they were ruled to be in violation of the law.

The Narcotic Drugs Import and Export Act of 1922, a federal statute, banned the import of refined products such as morphine and cocaine. Only the importation of crude drug material was permitted. In 1924, the importation of crude opium was banned as well.

In 1930 Congress established the Federal Bureau of Narcotics, a division of the Treasury Department with more clout than the drug enforcers had previously had. Shortly afterward, Harry J. Anslinger became director. Anslinger firmly believed in enforcement as the best remedy for most drug problems. He ran the agency for 32 years and made a strong mark on U.S. drug policy.

In 1937 Anslinger urged Congress to pass the Marijuana Tax Act, which restricted the legal use of marijuana to a few medical categories. Users were required to seek permission from the Treasury, pay a tax, and obtain a stamp as proof of payment. Possessing marijuana without a stamp became a federal crime.

Five years later Congress passed another drug-control law, the Opium Control Act, which outlawed the growing of opium poppies within the United States. During the 1940s, many states passed new laws or strengthened old ones forbidding the use of narcotics and marijuana. Many copied the federal statutes.

The 1950s saw the passage of two new federal laws — the Boggs Act of 1951 and the Narcotic Control Act of 1956.

The first act increased the mandatory minimum sentences for those convicted of selling or transporting marijuana, and the second law included some of the harshest penalties ever written. Judges were now enabled to impose the death penalty for anyone over 18 convicted of selling heroin to a minor.

In 1963 the Prettyman Commission, created by President John F. Kennedy, examined the federal government's entire attack on the problem of drug abuse and found it to be chaotic and in need of reform. It recommended that the government move away from mandatory punishment, emphasize medical treatment of addicts, and finance more research on the causes of addiction.

The First War on Drugs

Contemporary attitudes on drug use are rooted in events of the middle and late 1960s. The "baby boomers" born after World War II came into adolescence in this period. The war in Vietnam was escalating. American troops seemed unable to bring an end to the battle overseas, despite a massive deployment of troops and weapons. With each passing year, public opinion on the war became more sharply divided.

Teenagers were being sent to fight and die in an obscure nation in Southeast Asia. In the battle zone, soldiers were introduced to opium, heroin, and marijuana. Back at home, many adolescents who felt at odds with "the system" also became caught up in the drug fad. Dr. Timothy Leary, a researcher at Harvard who experimented with LSD and found it "consciousness-expanding," urged everyone to "tune in, turn on, drop out." Rock bands tuned in to this message, and often their lyrics reflected the feelings of alienation that seemed so common in the sixties, advertising a life-style that included drug use.

Marijuana was the drug of choice in the counterculture. Using it and defending its use became a part of the politics of dissent. Other hallucinogens also became popular at this time: LSD, mescaline, and almost anything that had mind-altering potential, including the seeds of the morning glory flower. In many inner-city neighborhoods, the drug of choice was heroin. Deaths from heroin overdose increased rapidly in the early 1970s before leveling off at the end of the decade.

President Lyndon Johnson and his administration viewed the restrictions against drug abuse as too lenient and established the Bureau of Narcotics and Dangerous Drugs in 1968. This agency was based in the Justice Department rather than the Treasury and organized as part of a strenuous police campaign against drug abuse.

President Richard Nixon came into office in 1969, inheriting the Vietnam War and the drug problem. He had promised to get U.S. troops out of Vietnam, and, in the meantime, he opened a "War on Drugs" at home. The federal budget for enforcement and research on drug abuse jumped from $81 million to $760 million in five years, a rise of 800%.

Nixon launched his war on drugs with a presidential message and government reorganization in June 1971. But a major step had already been taken the year before, when

Former Harvard psychology professor Timothy Leary encouraged many students to experiment with LSD and other drugs in the 1960s. In 1966, he appeared before 1,500 college students while experiencing psychedelic hallucinations.

Congress had passed the Comprehensive Drug Abuse Prevention and Control Act. The law was historically important because it provided a new, sweeping basis for federal police power. No longer did the government have to rely on the pretext of collecting taxes to prosecute illicit-drug use. Congress made it clear that unauthorized use of drugs, in and of itself, was a federal crime.

The act listed five "schedules" of drugs and ranked them according to the danger they posed to the public. The list included pharmaceuticals such as amphetamines and barbiturates, subjecting them to controls imposed on other dangerous drugs. The law also imposed a more orderly pattern on police administration.

The year after Nixon declared war on drugs, another important piece of legislation passed Congress: the Drug Abuse Office and Treatment Act of 1972. The law increased drug-police power, and a semblance of order was imposed on the rapidly expanding federal bureaucracy in this area. The law also greatly increased aid to addicts through treatment programs.

By way of treatment, the federal government supported a novel kind of clinic that "maintained" heroin addicts on a fixed regimen of methadone, which is a synthetic chemical that satisfies the addict's craving without providing the "high" of heroin. The goal was to stabilize drug use and reduce crime by providing a free fix, along with counseling. The number of federally funded drug treatment programs grew from 135 to 394 in 18 months. There was a slight irony in this decision, which resurrected in a modern form the old addict-treatment centers that had been forced to close in the period from 1919 to 1925.

In 1971 and 1972, the Nixon administration took steps to disrupt the international flow of drugs. The State Department won promises from foreign countries to prosecute illicit trade within their borders and gave economic aid in exchange. The goal was to stop the smuggling of drugs into the United States. It was thought that as much as 80% of United States street heroin came from Turkish poppy fields and made its way through French processing plants. Both Turkey and France agreed to cooperate, and by Nixon's second inauguration in January 1973, the "French Connection" was broken.

A patient at a drug rehabilitation center in Bangkok takes a prescribed dosage of the heroin substitute methadone. During the 1970s, many methadone clinics were established to treat heroin addiction in the United States.

A Brief Truce

In September 1973, Nixon effectively declared an end to his war on drugs. In a speech he said, "We have turned the corner on drug abuse in the United States." (Within a year, Nixon would resign his presidency in the wake of the Watergate scandals, revelations of widespread criminality on the part of his reelection staff.) Additional changes occurred in the 1970s after the great war on drugs, but none had the impact of actions taken between 1970 and 1973.

Some progress was made, however, in bringing bureaucratic confusion to an end. During the 1970s, police work was concentrated in the Drug Enforcement Administration (DEA), a part of the Justice Department. Medical treatment and research were centered in the National Institute on Drug

Abuse (NIDA), under the Department of Health and Human Services. This arrangement lasted, partly because drug problems stopped getting attention in the press, and politicians stopped redrawing the lines of authority. These two agencies play the leading roles in U.S. drug policy today.

The next two presidents — Gerald R. Ford and Jimmy Carter — declared no wars. They continued to stress the need for punishment of illicit drug dealers, but their approach was quieter. They remained low key, despite evidence that new drug sources had opened up in South and Central America, Mexico, and even (for marijuana) in remote areas of the United States.

Carter went so far as to suggest that the possession of small amounts of marijuana should be "decriminalized." This concept had already been espoused by the National Commission on Marijuana and Drug Abuse, a group appointed by the Nixon administration, though its officials never paid much attention to the committee's recommendations.

By "decriminalizing" marijuana, reformers hoped to lighten punishment for first-time and small-time users. Getting arrested for possession of marijuana, they said, should be akin to getting a traffic ticket. Reflecting the widespread if questionable view that marijuana was not addictive or terribly destructive, Carter said that "penalties against possession of a drug should not be more damaging to an individual than the use of the drug itself." The reason for letting small-time users off the hook was that this would allow the police to concentrate on the "hard" drugs and major dealers. Minor offenders would be treated, not punished.

Other intellectual and political leaders took up the cause of decriminalization. A report financed by the Ford Foundation, *Dealing with Drug Abuse*, claimed that large scale enforcement was bound to fail. It called for a more sophisticated attack on addiction, urging more research on treatment and prevention. After the report's release in 1972, the Ford Foundation decided to support a staff in Washington to carry out some of the recommendations. During its seven years of operation, the Drug Abuse Council fostered the view, as it said in its final report in 1980, that "severe criminal sanctions against the use of small amounts of marijuana are neither appropriate nor effective."

Although the federal government never officially adopted this view, some states did. Eleven decided to reduce the penalties for possessing a small amount of marijuana (less than one ounce). These softer laws remain in effect today in Alaska, California, Colorado, Minnesota, Mississippi, Nebraska, New York, North Carolina, and Oregon. No state went so far as to make marijuana legal. In the November 1986 election, Oregon voters had a chance to legalize the drug in a state referendum but decided against it.

New York State softened the penalty for possessing a small amount of marijuana but also enacted a "get tough" law that imposed mandatory sentences for possessing large, dealer-sized quantities of drugs. The mandatory sentences did not work well, and after several years they were abandoned. The courts were clogged with cases, and ultimately the police became the real arbiters of justice, arresting only those who made a good case by police standards. Neither the "soft" nor the "hard" laws had a significant impact on the rate of addiction in the states that adopted these new legal approaches.

The Second War On Drugs

In the early morning of June 19, 1986, Len Bias, a young basketball star at the University of Maryland, died of a cocaine overdose. It was a sensational case, making headlines across the country. Bias was a black scholarship student, a campus leader, and a model of success for other impoverished young athletes. The fact that he was involved with drugs at all came as a shock. Then, eight days later, a professional football player, Don Rogers, also died from cocaine use.

Although this double blow was not the sole stimulus for the new battle against drug abuse, it did serve as the immediate trigger. The federal government, in a joint attack involving President Ronald Reagan and Congress, declared a second war on drugs and passed a major new drug law in the fall of 1986.

Interestingly, the rates of drug use had not changed at all. What was new was that marijuana use had tapered off, while cocaine use had grown. A significant new element in this development was the wide availability of crack, a concentrated, smokable version of cocaine that could be pur-

President Reagan signs into law the Anti-Drug Abuse Act of 1986. The law, which sets stricter penalties for those convicted of drug crimes, aims to stop illicit drug production.

chased in small quantities. It has been described as the most intensely addicting chemical ever to appear on the drug scene.

Long before the crisis hit, President Reagan had taken steps to move the federal government away from decriminalization and back toward a strict enforcement approach to drug abuse. In October 1982, the White House released a "Federal Strategy for Prevention of Drug Abuse and Drug Trafficking." Using strong words, it proposed a more vigorous and better-coordinated attack on drug dealers. But, coming in a time of tight budgets, it provided no increase in funding and suggested no dramatic change in the law.

The Reagan administration did set up a number of antidrug strike squads, beginning with the South Florida Task Force in 1982, which was headed by Vice-president George

Bush. Also in 1982, all federal drug agents — including those in the Drug Enforcement Administration — were brought under the direction of the FBI. In 1983, 12 additional task forces, including one for each region of the country, were created to coordinate a war on drug traffic. At the same time, the president and Congress authorized the use of U.S. military troops and equipment in overseas battles against drug producers, notably in Colombia. Other legal changes increased the government's ability to use confidential personal data on drug dealers and to seize their property.

These early Reagan administration actions were dwarfed, however, by the crisis legislation passed on October 17, 1986. Known as the Anti-Drug Abuse Act, the new law provided $1.7 billion for the federal government's new drug war. Most of the increase ($500 million) went to pay for "drug interdiction" by the Department of Defense and the Coast Guard. Remaining funds were directed toward federal enforcement ($275 million), state and local police ($230 million), treatment and rehabilitation ($241 million), and prevention programs ($200 million). Congress came close to imposing the death penalty for certain drug offenses but stopped short. It did enact some mandatory sentencing requirements, however, including a minimum fine of $1,000 to be imposed on people caught with a small amount of illicit drugs.

When President Reagan signed the bill into law, he took federal policy back to an earlier era. It was in the 1950s that mandatory federal penalties for narcotics use were originally tried.

Whether this massive enforcement will work any better in the 1980s than it did 30 years ago is an open question. On the one hand, the record suggests that the enforcers have made some new promises that will be very difficult to keep. On the other, recent evidence concerning the dangers of certain illicit drugs — and some startling statistics linking drug use and trafficking with other serious crimes — suggests that the renewed war against drugs is a battle worth fighting.

Al Capone controlled Chicago's bootlegging, as well as its illegal gambling network, during the Prohibition years. His illicit liquor business brought in an estimated $3.6 billion per year.

CHAPTER 2

ALCOHOL: THE LEGAL DRUG

For 13 years (1920–1933), the United States tried to fight alcoholism by outlawing the sale of liquor, wine, and beer. It was a losing battle. The campaign never had the full support of the federal government or the nation's cultural leaders. Even with a united leadership, it would have been hard to change drinking patterns that had developed over centuries. But the nation was not in agreement, and the law was widely violated.

In time, Prohibition came to be seen not just as a failure but as a desperate and foolish mistake. Today, many people who oppose controls on "recreational" drugs — particularly controls on marijuana — cite Prohibition as evidence that it is futile to try to outlaw a popular intoxicant. The heart of this argument is that, even if it were desirable in theory, prohibition cannot be carried out in practice. People will find a way to get what they want, the argument goes, and outlawing a drug merely sends drug seekers into an illegal black market.

This may sound reasonable. But it raises some interesting questions. For example, just why did Prohibition fail? Was it truly a disaster? Did it increase crime? Did it actually cause more people to become alcoholics, as is sometimes suggested? Finally, just how valid is the analogy that compares modern drug use to alcohol consumption in the 1920s?

Franklin Delano Roosevelt (second from right) proposed making liquor legal again immediately after being elected president in 1932. One year later, Prohibition was repealed.

Upon entering the White House in 1932, Franklin Delano Roosevelt immediately proposed making beer legal again. Voters liked the idea, and it soon became clear in state elections that many were ready for a total repeal of the Prohibition laws. By the end of Roosevelt's first year in office, enough states had voted in favor of repealing the 18th Amendment that it was removed from the books. In 1933 Roosevelt happily put a stake through the heart of what he called the "damnable affliction of Prohibition." Alcohol in all its forms became legal again, and for many, Roosevelt's campaign song summed it up: "Happy Days Are Here Again."

Although Prohibition was dead, the heat of the political battle remained for a long time. People who wrote about it often saw things as the winners did. The winners, of course, were the proalcohol forces, including groups such as the Association Against the Prohibition Amendment. They denounced Prohibition as creating hypocrisy in government, gangsterism, bribery, and — not least of its crimes — bad liquor. "Alcohol and Al Capone," one historian said, "became the twin villains of the era." Many believed Prohibition had given birth to a crime wave and helped bring on the economic depression that began in 1929.

The proliquor movement also had support in the late 1920s from leaders of big business eager to offset their own new income-tax burdens with fees collected from the sale of liquor. As long as liquor was illegal, it could not be taxed. Distillers and brewers lobbied to end Prohibition, for obvious reasons.

These opponents argued that the law was based on out-dated moral codes. They saw it as an attempt to force a narrow view of correct behavior on the whole society. It was bound to fail, they said. Newspaper cartoonists often poked fun at the Prohibitionists, depicting them as black-suited, cranky spinsters and preachers.

As recently as 1960, a major study on the subject described the antialcohol movement as a desperate last gasp of Puritanism and an attempt to turn back the clock. In contrast, the campaign to bring back liquor came to stand for values of normality and sanity. By throwing off the chains of Prohibition, it was argued, America could transcend its puritanical past and join the community of civilized nations.

A 1921 photograph shows state troopers arresting a bootlegger. Many opponents of Prohibition saw it as an overly moralistic amendment.

Prohibition in a New Light

Recently, a new understanding of Prohibition has emerged. Alcoholism, it is now clear, is an enduring national affliction. As recognition of the size of the problem has grown, people have begun to see alcohol abuse as a form of drug abuse. And as scholars have gained detachment from the battles of the 1920s, they also gained sympathy for the antiliquor crusaders of those years.

In the 1980s, the data show that alcohol and nicotine addiction are the major drug-related causes of disease and early death among Americans. The toll on the family, on public safety, and on national productivity is significant. The crusaders of the 19th century stressed alcohol's power to break down personal character, to rot the brain, and destroy the family. These old themes of the temperance leaders might not seem so out of place today, as evidence of alcohol's effects on the brain and on family life are documented with growing clarity.

A meeting of researchers on alcoholism held at the University of California at San Diego in 1987 showed the disease was responsible for a litany of suffering and loss. According to a 1987 article in *Science* magazine, about $13.5 million is spent each year directly on treatment of alcoholics. The national economy also suffers losses to alcoholism through accidents, sickness, and slack productivity — by one guess, about $117 billion a year.

Enoch Gordis, director of the National Institute on Alcoholism and Alcohol Abuse, estimated that 25 to 40% of the patients in hospitals on any given day are suffering from alcohol-related problems. These include diseases of the liver and heart, gastrointestinal disorders, and psychiatric ailments. Studies show that active alcoholics require hospital services about four times as frequently as nonalcoholics, and their families need medical care about twice as often as other families.

Along with the new concern about alcohol abuse came a desire to reinvestigate earlier efforts to control drinking. Those who looked into the record found that the accomplishments of Prohibition were not always as small as the repealers claimed, and its faults were not as large. Two commonly accepted ideas that have proved to be wrong or insubstantial are the notion that Prohibition really did not begin to reduce the availability of liquor and that its cost to society in terms of increased crime was greater than its benefit in reducing alcohol-related problems.

Some scholars now point out that per-capita consumption of alcohol went down during Prohibition. According to a 1968 estimate by T. C. Burnham, it declined from 1.69 gallons per person a year to 0.98 gallons during World War I (1918–1919). It then fell further, to 0.73 gallons (1921–1922), before rising to 1.14 gallons just as Prohibition was repealed.

The statistics on death and hospitalization tell more, for they are the strongest indicators of the actual level of alcohol abuse. According to a 1981 study by David Musto, the rate of death from cirrhosis of the liver among men dropped from 29.5 per 100,000 in 1911 to 10.7 in 1929 — a significant decrease. The number of state mental hospital admissions per 100,000 classified as "alcoholic psychosis" dropped from 10.1 in 1919 to 3.7 in 1922, rising again to 4.7 in 1928. In

A cartoon satirizes Prohibition. The ban on alcohol caused sales of coffee and soft drinks to soar.

New York state, the admission rate to state mental hospitals in 1920 was about one-fifth as large as in the period from 1909 to 1912. Remarkably, arrests for drunkenness in this period declined 50%.

The investigator Eliot Ness and his band of special agents, known as the "untouchables," have given us a dramatic image of Chicago's corruption by the illegal liquor industry, but in retrospect, historians now believe, there was no upsurge in crime in the 1920s. The black market in liquor did bring corruption but not enough to affect the statistics. According to Burnham, "no statistics from this period dealing with crime are of any value whatsoever in generalizing about crime rates. Apparently what happened was that in the 1920s the long existent 'underworld' first became publicized and romanticized. The crime wave, in other words, was the invention of enterprising journalists. . . . " Many disagree with this view, arguing that organized crime really gained a foothold in American life during the 1920s by supplying illegal liquor.

But it is safe to say the record of Prohibition is more complex than popular reporting has made clear. The campaign did fail, but not without some accomplishments.

Alcohol vs. Drug Laws

The failure of Prohibition has been taken as a sign that any attempt to control intoxicants will be doomed. But it is worth asking why the ban on alcohol failed. Was the law written badly or administered badly? Did it prove physically impossible to end the use of a popular drug? Is there something special about alcohol that makes it harder to control than other chemicals? Or are the controls on other drugs — marijuana, cocaine, and heroin — destined to the same failure as Prohibition?

Social historians give several explanations for the collapse of Prohibition, in contrast to the continued enforcement of narcotics laws. But the majority of them believe that the most important difference between alcohol and the drugs banned by the Harrison Act of 1914 lies in their places in American cultural tradition.

People have used alcohol since the earliest moments of recorded history. The technology for making it is ancient, and its use is an integral part of Western customs, art, and

Americans celebrated the repeal of Prohibition in style in December 1933. Social historians believe that the amendment failed because it attempted to eliminate an integral part of Western culture.

literature. Heroin and purified cocaine, in contrast, are the products of a new expertise in chemistry that arose in the 19th century. Until recently, chemical drugs were an oddity and a rarity. Their use was not a part of the American social scene.

It is true that opium and marijuana have a long tradition of social use in other cultures. But they were not used by the Europeans who settled the American colonies. During the colonial period, alcoholic drinks, in contrast, were regarded by many as a healthy part of the common diet. In later years, alcohol retained its social status as a boon to festivity, but other drugs, such as opium, never achieved the same level of social acceptance and at best were seen as something to be kept in the medicine cabinet.

Opium was also associated with poor immigrant Chinese, who came to the United States in large numbers during the 19th century seeking work. They took the lowliest and hardest jobs on the docks and the new railroads, and they brought along a taste for opium. The "opium dens" of San Francisco became notorious as centers of low-life and crime. Marijuana also came to be associated with down-and-outers. It was used by Mexican-American laborers and later came to be seen, along with cocaine, as a drug used by blacks. Musto writes that at the time of Prohibition, many believed that opiates and cocaine made users insane and violent. These drugs "were widely . . . associated with foreigners or alien subgroups." Many feared that "use of all these drugs was spreading into the 'higher classes.' " Thus, legislators, supported by many leading members of society, during the early part of the 20th century felt confident in their decision to outlaw the recreational use of narcotics and cocaine.

This was not the case with alcohol. Even during Prohibition, about half the nation, according to surveys, believed that the use of alcohol in moderation was acceptable. Another big difference between the ban on drugs and the ban on drinking was that the use of alcohol was supported by social leaders, but the use of drugs was not. This helps explain why Prohibition never succeeded.

A half-heartedness can be found in the law itself and in the way it was enforced. Although the Prohibition amendment outlawed the manufacture, transportation, and sale of alcohol, it did allow people to possess alcohol. People who could afford to bought stocks of liquor before the law went into effect and were able to drink legally through the dry years. Poorer people could not. The law also allowed people to make small quantities of wine and beer at home for family use, a loophole that came to be widely exploited.

Finally, historians believe that the federal government provided insufficient funds to enforce prohibition effectively. This neglect may have come about in an attempt to keep costs down, or it may have been part of a general reluctance to play the intrusive role of party-killer. For example, in 1920 the U.S. government had only about 1,500 agents to enforce Prohibition throughout the nation, and many of them were poorly trained political appointees. The force was rife with corruption and incompetence. In general, the states were no more eager than Washington to spend money on a crusade that lacked full public support.

Other factors may have helped kill Prohibition. It has been said that in the wake of the stock market crash of 1929 and the ensuing economic crisis, the furor over alcohol seemed trivial. In addition, a new generation began moving into power, and the new leaders did not care to fight every battle started by their elders. Even conservatives who might once have sympathized with alcohol controls began to see Prohibition as government meddling with private life.

The tide turned, and a nation that had never really put its heart into the Prohibition crusade in the first place finally gave up on it.

Some Lessons

As the statistics show, the campaign against alcohol was not a total failure. The rate of drinking did go down, particularly among the poorer classes. Incidences of cirrhosis and other diseases of the heavy drinker tapered off. Clearly, the reduction in alcohol's availability had some good results. But at the same time, the law created a new and illegal trade that the government could not control. This led to cynicism, further weakening the enforcement effort.

Prohibition seems to have reflected more a wish than a commitment, for as we have said the nation never backed the law with enough funds to carry out its enforcement. The attempt to ban certain drugs has been more successful because public support for enforcement has been stronger and the social acceptance of these drugs much weaker. Finally, national leaders have not been divided on how to handle these drugs, as they had been on alcohol.

The record suggests that laws banning an intoxicant will succeed to the extent that they represent what the public and its leaders really want. Such laws also require a vigorous effort at enforcement if they are to succeed. Obviously, the more widespread the use of the drug, the bigger the enforcement cost will be. Even if the enforcement is not perfect, it may still reduce the availability of an intoxicant, with some beneficial effects. Prohibition is likely to fail when the use of the outlawed drug is widespread and widely accepted, and when the enforcement effort is too small to keep up with the illegal trade.

Basketball star Len Bias, first-round draft choice of the Boston Celtics, posed with Celtic coach K.C. Jones in 1986. Two days after the photograph was taken, Bias died from an overdose of cocaine.

CHAPTER 3

DRUG ABUSE TODAY: TRENDS AND CONSEQUENCES

No one knows the true number of illicit drug users or the quantity of drugs they buy in the United States. It is a secret business, and no one gives out official records. Any discussion of this subject is contingent on educated guesses. Some methods of guessing are better than others, but all work by taking samples of behavior in a survey, and using samples to predict the behavior of the whole nation.

One way to take a sample is to go directly to the market and ask questions. Obviously, drug dealers are not a good source of information; they have much to hide and little to gain by talking about their trade. But users are not as reluctant, and fortunately many will discuss their experiences if approached as part of a general survey. Their cooperation is crucial in providing the picture of drug use discussed below.

The National Institute on Drug Abuse (NIDA) has several ways of watching the drug market. The most important of these are a survey of 5,600 homes across the country (begun in 1971) and a survey of 16,000 high school seniors (begun in 1975).

Two problems with these surveys should be mentioned. One is that people tend to say they use drugs less than they really do. This is especially true in the 1980s, when drug use

The National Institute on Drug Abuse, headed by Dr. Charles Schuster, studies the consequences of drug abuse on society by examining both the effects of the substances and the behavior of abusers.

has been looked on less favorably than it had been 10 years earlier. The second is that it is probable that the heaviest adolescent drug users drop out of high school before they would become seniors and are therefore not surveyed. The result is that estimates based on these surveys make the drug trade seem smaller than it is. But because these surveys seem to reflect trends of drug use accurately, they are very good at showing general patterns of change.

Good information also comes in reports from hospitals and medical examiners across the country on the number of drug-related deaths and visits to emergency rooms. These data are collected by the Drug Abuse Warning Network (DAWN). Treatment centers also give some anonymous information. Finally, the police collect information on the amount of drugs they seize, including purity, origin, and the price being charged by dealers. A good summary of this data is the Narcotics Intelligence Estimate 1984, published by the U.S. Drug Enforcement Administration in Washington, D.C.

Taken together, these clues provide a fairly clear picture of the nation's drug habits over the last 20 years. Many are alarmed by what they see. There can be no doubt that the use of illegal drugs, which seemed to be a minor problem in the 1950s, exploded in the 1960s and 1970s with an epidemic of heroin addiction and an enormous expansion in marijuana use. Heroin seems to have lost its popularity since then, and marijuana use has tapered off somewhat as well. But all the signs indicate that cocaine is moving in to take the place of earlier favorites.

In the new form known as "crack," which is easily converted to a potent vapor during smoking, cocaine has become a major drug abuse problem. Its impact may be even greater than that of the heroin epidemic of the 1960s because it does not seem to carry the same negative image as heroin — or did not until recently.

Each drug in the illicit market is sold and used in its own distinctive fashion. Below are sketches of the historical trends for three major drugs. They reflect data from sources mentioned above and reports by several NIDA scientists.

Trends in Drug Use

Heroin

When the first narcotics laws were passed, the number of heroin addicts in the United States was significant but probably smaller than the number police officials gave. For example, it is now estimated that in the 1920s, there were not "millions" of addicts, as claimed, but perhaps 100,000. Early estimates were not reliable. But later estimates make it clear that heroin use grew dramatically in the late 1960s. This epidemic was linked to servicemen returning from Vietnam, who brought home a taste for a drug that was easy to obtain in Southeast Asia. A wave of concern about heroin prompted the Nixon administration's "War on Drugs" in the early 1970s (see Chapter 1).

According to information from drug treatment centers, the number of people who said they had just recently become addicted declined sharply after 1970. Another sharp drop in the number of new addicts occurred in 1975. This group is now described as an "aging population," a remnant of the epidemic years. Most observers think the number of heroin addicts in the United States has settled somewhere between 400,000 and 600,000, and that these are primarily "old" addicts who began taking the drug in the 1970s. Some research indicates that during the peak years, the number of nonaddicted, or "controlled," users may have been much larger, perhaps seven times more. These users take heroin carefully, in the way a moderate drinker has a cocktail a few times a week.

There appears to have been no major change in the level of heroin consumption in the United States since 1981. The number of heroin-related hospital emergency visits has de-

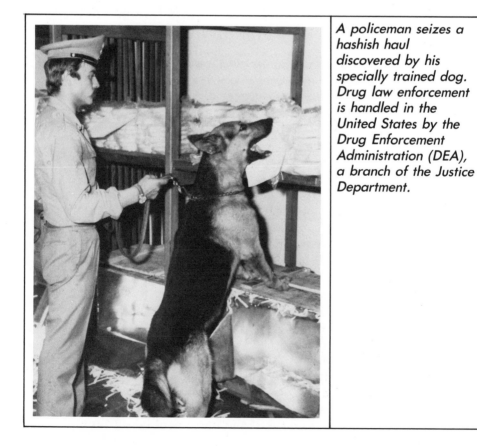

A policeman seizes a hashish haul discovered by his specially trained dog. Drug law enforcement is handled in the United States by the Drug Enforcement Administration (DEA), a branch of the Justice Department.

This British woman was arrested by Egyptian authorities in connection with a heroin smuggling attempt. Britain requires that heroin addicts register with the state and report regularly to medical clinics.

clined, but the number of deaths has increased from 698 in 1981 to 1,005 in 1984. Most of these deaths resulted from the use of heroin in combination with another drug, such as alcohol.

Despite a massive international effort to break up the heroin trade, no progress has been made in reducing the drug's availability. Enforcement officials report that the price of heroin went down, meaning that the amount in the market went up. Its purity also increased between 1981 and 1984.

Britain, which also experienced a massive upsurge in the use of heroin during the 1960s, faced a different kind of problem. Up until that time, doctors in the United Kingdom were permitted to prescribe all painkillers — including heroin and morphine — without interference from legal authorities. Unfortunately, many of these doctors abused this privilege, leading to a series of drug prescription scandals, and to a dramatic increase in the number of heroin addicts. Britain introduced a new system in 1967 that required all heroin addicts to register with the state. In return, they were given free access to drugs, but only by reporting regularly to medical clinics, where they were regarded as outpatients.

The system has received mixed reviews. On the one hand, the number of registered addicts has grown rather slowly, apparently stabilizing at around 3,000. Britain seems to have contained its heroin problem. On the other hand, some critics of the program say that the clinics have become so unappealing to addicts that many have gone outside the system to find drugs on the street. Most observers feel, however, that Britain has avoided the worst of the drug epidemic that appeared in Europe, or in the United States.

Marijuana

The increase in marijuana use by high-school students that occurred in the late 1960s and 1970s reflected a radical change in attitude toward drugs other than alcohol and is likely to have an impact for many years to come. In the 1950s, the number of teenagers smoking marijuana was "minuscule," according to William Pollin, a recent director of NIDA. But, by the end of the 1970s, astonishingly, 11% of high school seniors said they were using marijuana every day. Since then, the drug's popularity has declined, and less than half as many — about 5% — report using it daily. Similarly, in 1975 about 27% said they had used marijuana sometime in the previous month. By 1978, the monthly users grew to 37%; this figure dropped to 23% in 1986.

The household survey indicates that about 62 million Americans have used this illegal drug at least once. But the number of 12 to 17 year olds who report using it within the last month has dropped from a high point of 17% in 1979 to around 12% in 1987. This is still a significant share of the U.S. population, indicating that there is an abiding and widespread willingness to violate the narcotics laws.

At last count, 11 states had completely eliminated jail sentences for possession of a small amount of marijuana. Many retain strong penalties for possessing larger quantities, on the assumption that only dealers would keep such stocks on hand, and that dealers must be punished. This movement toward decriminalizing marijuana, which began in the mid-1970s, has had no noticeable impact on consumption. A recent review

56

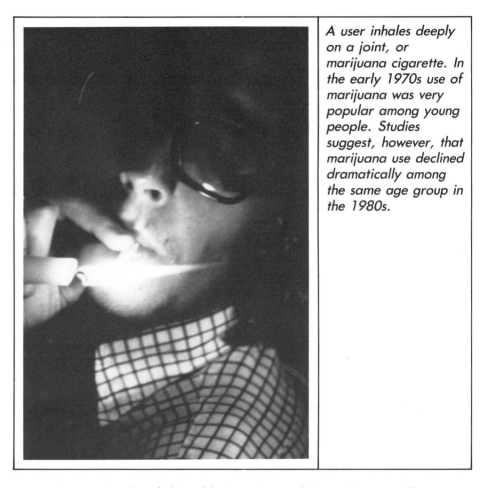

A user inhales deeply on a joint, or marijuana cigarette. In the early 1970s use of marijuana was very popular among young people. Studies suggest, however, that marijuana use declined dramatically among the same age group in the 1980s.

by Eric Single of the Addiction Research Foundation in Toronto concludes, "In those areas in which the effects of decriminalization were monitored, there appears to have been a minimal impact on rates of marijuana use but a reduction in the social costs associated with the enforcement of the marijuana laws."

Cocaine

There is a significant link between cocaine and marijuana. Marijuana is sometimes called a "gateway" drug that often leads to the abuse of more potent chemicals. In one recent survey, it is interesting to note that most "high-risk cocaine abusers" said they had already used marijuana for 10 years.

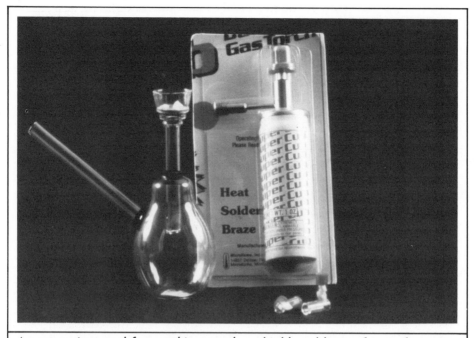

A water pipe used for smoking crack, a highly addictive form of cocaine. Abuse of crack has become widespread in the 1980s.

This does not mean that marijuana smoking inevitably causes cocaine use, but it does mean that longtime marijuana use may be associated with other kinds of addiction.

As heroin and marijuana use declines in the 1980s, the popularity of cocaine seems to be on the rise. As recently as 1975, cocaine was not thought of as dangerous or addictive. The view of cocaine has changed radically since then. Scientists have discovered that the drug is in fact highly addictive. As William Pollin notes, it is the "one drug that animals do not have to be trained to use," and it is "the one drug that animals consistently choose in preference to food and water, to the point of death." A particularly dangerous form of cocaine is crack, which is thought not only to produce addiction but to produce it faster than any other drug. Pollin believes that because of the growing availability of inexpensive crack, the nation may be about to confront the most serious drug problem it has ever experienced.

More than 22 million Americans are thought to have used cocaine at least once, a dramatic increase from the 5.4 million who had tried it in 1974. The number who use it at least once a month has grown from 1.6 million in 1977 to 5.8 million in 1985. The percentage of surveyed high school seniors who said they had used cocaine in the last month tripled from about 2% in 1975 to 6% in 1985. There is some evidence that the peak period is ending, however, because the percentage of high school seniors who reported using cocaine within 30 days declined in 1986.

The medical data also point to a crisis. The number of cocaine-related hospital emergencies increased threefold — from 3,296 to 9,946 per year — between 1981 and 1985. Deaths rose from 195 to 580 per year.

Law enforcement campaigns to break up the cocaine trade have been spectacular in recent years, and the quantity of cocaine seized by authorities has grown by more than 400% since 1982. But the impact on the black market has been small. The price of cocaine has actually declined, and federal officials report that the quantity of cocaine available to users has more than doubled since 1982. The new method of selling cocaine as crack may have alarming implications for the future, some say. It permits dealers to peddle the drug in small quantities of $10 each, whereas in the past the minimum "buy" was about $100. The new trend makes cocaine much more affordable for the young and the poor, the ones most likely to be hurt by it.

Cost to the Individual of Using Drugs

Many people feel that the worst consequence of becoming hooked on a drug is the dependence itself. It is seen as a loss of control over one's own fate, a failure of will, or surrender to forces of destruction and chaos. Addictive drugs are said to make a person into a slave or deprive the user of freedom. This is seen as an evil in itself.

It is difficult to analyze this aspect of drug abuse. But it is a familiar complaint and one that many people think is important. Scientists have had trouble defining exactly what addiction is, but it is clear that some people can use drugs without being addicts or abusers.

Technically, there is a difference between addiction (compulsive and continued harmful use of a drug) and the more specific problem of physical dependence (physical tolerance for increased doses of a drug, followed by a certain behavior if the drug is withdrawn). Heroin, for example, causes addiction and physical dependence. Tolerance occurs in heroin users because the body's chemistry adjusts to the presence of a drug that blocks nerve signals and produces euphoric effects. Ever larger quantities of heroin are needed to achieve the pleasurable effect. Withdrawal of heroin after a long period of use stimulates a well-recognized pattern of nervous activity and flulike symptoms. This pattern stops in 7 to 10 days. Some drugs that are addictive, such as cocaine, may not produce physical dependence in lab animals. This subject is being investigated.

What is the difference between an addict and a moderate user? It is hard to find clear answers to this question. It is possible that some people are more prone than others to addiction. The former may experience a more euphoric high after taking a psychoactive substance, and for that reason they may have more intense cravings after the drug's effects have worn off. Some researchers believe that biochemical makeup, certain personality traits, or both can determine, at least in part, whether a person is likely to become addicted. Genetic factors may also play a role. In the case of alcohol, for example, it has been proven that the children of problem drinkers have a greater chance of becoming alcoholics themselves. This could very well hold true in the case of other potentially addicting drugs as well. But the same person may be addicted first to one, then to a different kind of drug, even if the substances have clashing physiological effects.

For example, heroin is a depressant. When it kills, it generally does so by slowing the rate of breathing until the flow of oxygen to the body ceases. Cocaine, by contrast, is a stimulant. When it kills, it does so by overstimulation, often causing damage to the heart or interfering with breathing. Both drugs are addictive, and there is no evidence that people become hooked on just one or the other type. On the contrary, many addicts switch from one to the other. Some use both at once, in a concoction known as a "speedball."

Even harder than guessing the number of drug users in the United States is guessing how many of them are addicts.

A rough guide, based on a careful analysis of alcohol users, is that 1 out of every 10 users may be likely to have serious problems that are directly related to his or her compulsive use of a drug. Others have suggested that the ratio of addicts to users may be higher for crack and heroin — perhaps as high as one addict for every seven users, or even one for every four. But these proportions have not been clearly established. For the purpose of this discussion, it is safe to assume that 1 in every 10 users has a serious problem with the drug.

Certainly, the worst effect of any drug is death. Alcohol is thought to kill directly more than 30,000 people a year, either by poisoning or by causing cirrhosis of the liver. (This

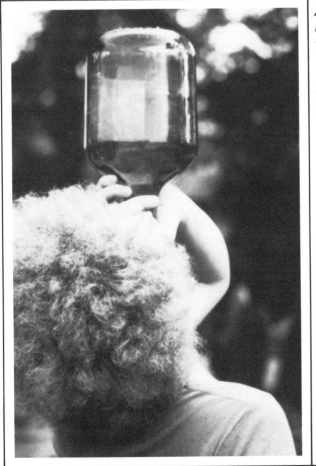

Although alcohol remains a legal and widely accepted drug, it is responsible for more than 30,000 deaths in the United States each year.

does not reflect the harrowing number of deaths caused by drunk driving.) Alcohol in combination with other drugs kills more than 1,300 (not counting New York City, which has recently had trouble collecting data). Heroin accounts for about 1,300 deaths. Cocaine accounts for more than 660. Heroin with cocaine kills more than 225. Although marijuana smoking alone is not usually lethal, 24 reported deaths in 1985 were caused by a combination of marijuana and another drug.

Hazardous to Your Health

The chemicals in marijuana are known as cannabinoids, a general term for the 421 (the number identified so far) to 1,000 compounds found in the *cannabis sativa* plant. The compound that most affects perception is called delta-9-tetra-hydrocannabinol (THC), an oily substance that does not dissolve in water. It affects the brain in ways that are still not clearly understood.

Alcohol dissolves in water and is quickly flushed out by metabolic functions. THC, however, has a relatively long residence time in the body and can be stored in fatty tissue. According to a recent report from the National Institute on Drug Abuse, marijuana has a half-life of 50 hours. In other words, it takes the body more than two days to remove half the THC present, as compared with one hour for alcohol. Cocaine has a half-life of more than one hour. Because marijuana's half-life is so long, it means that regular users may be continuously exposed to THC. There is also evidence that THC may accumulate in the brain.

There is no consensus that marijuana causes physical dependence, but some researchers believe that it does. According to Forest Tennant, M.D. of the Community Health Project of Los Angeles, users of high-potency marijuana (marijuana with a high THC content) show withdrawal symptoms about a week after they stop using the drug.

In the short term, smoking marijuana causes an increase in heart rate and a reddening of the eyes due to dilation of blood vessels. Several studies have shown that intoxication with marijuana blunts reflexes and makes the user clumsy — a dangerous effect for anyone driving a car, riding a motorcycle, or flying an airplane. One study indicates that the impact on performance can last eight hours. In addition, researchers have concluded that marijuana intoxication impairs memory and hinders perception in a way that retards the learning process. Long-term use or heavy use in adolescence may damage intellectual and emotional development.

There have been conflicting reports concerning the effects of marijuana on the reproductive system, but there is some evidence that women who take the drug during pregnancy have a greater likelihood of giving birth to premature, low-birth-weight, or malformed babies. Although the results have not been confirmed by studies on humans, there is strong evidence that long-term, regular use of marijuana can reduce the effectiveness of the immune system and make a person more vulnerable to the entire spectrum of infective agents, including the common cold.

Cocaine is a water-soluble salt, a stimulant that the body eliminates in a matter of a few hours. In its 1984 report to Congress, NIDA says that cocaine appears to be addictive and users who quit the drug "cold turkey" suffer withdrawal symptoms such as nausea and hallucinations.

Without question, cocaine is lethal. The deaths in 1986 of Len Bias and Don Rogers (see Chapter 1) drove home a point already established in medicine: Overdosing on cocaine can kill. Cocaine causes potentially fatal disturbances in the heart's rhythm. In the short term, exposure to cocaine increases the heart rate and blood pressure. There is some evidence from animal studies that cocaine may damage the liver as well. Large doses also affect mental stability, and may produce a pattern of behavior that closely resembles paranoid schizophrenia.

The information on marijuana and cocaine, the two most popular illicit drugs, serves to illustrate the typical health problems drug use can precipitate in the individual. Now let us take a brief look at the costs society encounters as a result of widespread drug abuse.

Costs to Society of Drug Abuse

There are no records on what drug abuse costs the nation, just as there are no official records on the amount of drugs sold or the number of addicts. But some thoughtful estimates have been made. One recent study of this question was per-

Cleveland Browns football star Don Rogers (left) died from cocaine abuse in 1986. Many sports teams have introduced drug testing in response to the growing problem of drug abuse among athletes.

formed by a group of four analysts (Henrick J. Harwood, Diane M. Napolitano, Patricia L. Kristiansen, and James J. Collins) in 1984 at the Research Triangle Institute (RTI) in Research Triangle Park, North Carolina. Using data collected through 1980, they estimated the cost to the nation of alcohol abuse, drug abuse, and mental health problems. They divided the results into "core costs" (those related to health care and loss of productivity) and "other related costs" (those having to do with the criminal justice system.)

The RTI analysts found that the nation lost $79.6 billion in "core costs" because of alcohol abuse in 1980. And it lost another $29.4 billion because of drug abuse. If the cost of crime and law enforcement are added in, the total comes to $89.5 billion for alcohol and $46.9 billion for drug abuse.

One of the questions to be considered in the legalization debate is whether the cost to society — especially the cost of crime and law enforcement — would be lessened if certain illicit drugs were made legally available. It is one of the issues discussed at length in Chapters 5 and 6, which present, respectively, the cases for and against the legalization of marijuana. The next chapter discusses legal uses of some illicit psychoactive drugs of which many people may not be aware.

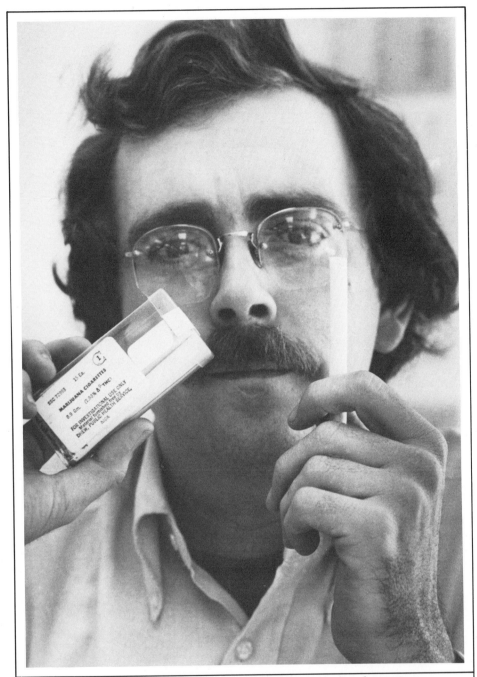

Glaucoma patient Robert Randall displays a supply of marijuana cigarettes. Randall smokes marijuana regularly — and legally — to relieve the pressure in his eyes caused by his disease.

CHAPTER 4

ILLICIT DRUGS AS MEDICINE

Once a month, Robert Randall goes to a pharmacy in Washington, D.C., and collects a silvery can that is waiting for him. It comes from the National Institute on Drug Abuse (NIDA) and contains about 300 neatly packed marijuana cigarettes. The government intends Randall to smoke this drug, which is cultivated on a farm run by the federal government in Mississippi and processed under federal contract. Randall is entitled to it because it eases the pain caused by his illness, glaucoma. He won the right to this "marijuana therapy" with the help of his lawyers, who carved out an exception to the law.

Glaucoma is a progressive disease of the eye and optic disc that often results in blindness. Randall learned in the early 1970s that he had glaucoma and by accident discovered that smoking marijuana relieved the pressure in his eyes. Randall also takes standard medicine for his glaucoma. He now has only about 10% of normal vision, but he claims that his condition stabilized when he began smoking marijuana regularly. This is not based on his own idle theory but rather on a well-documented effect of marijuana. Several studies since 1971 have shown that smoking marijuana causes the pressure within the eye to decrease and to remain at a lowered level for about five hours. One must keep smoking at regular intervals to sustain the effect.

Randall is the only person in the United States who regularly receives legal marijuana cigarettes and has done so for a long time — about 15 years. Randall does not pay for the marijuana he receives, even though he has offered to do so. The government does not want to put itself in the awkward position of selling marijuana, an illegal activity.

There may be as many as 2 million glaucoma victims in the United States. Randall has formed an organization called Alliance for Cannabis Therapeutics (ACT) that is lobbying for the legal use of marijuana as medicine. According to ACT, 10 to 20% of glaucoma patients might benefit from smoking marijuana. The drawback, of course, is that marijuana smoking also causes intoxication, and not everyone wants to get high. Prolonged use of marijuana may present other risks, such as increasing the odds of getting lung cancer and damaging the reproductive and immune systems (see Chapter 3). Eye doctors have not been eager to experiment with marijuana either,

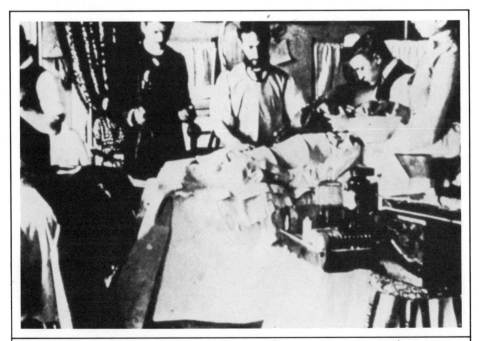

This 1850 photograph depicts a doctor administering an anesthetic to a patient before an operation. Use of drugs for therapeutic purposes dates back to the 4th century B.C.E.

according to the government official in charge of approving applications for experimental use of marijuana.

Doctors may not normally prescribe marijuana because it is listed as a Schedule I drug, the most forbidden category under the 1970 Federal Controlled Substances Act. This category includes drugs that, according to drug enforcement and health agencies, have "no currently accepted medical use" but have great potential for misuse. Among the items listed as Schedule I drugs are marijuana, heroin, and LSD (lysergic acid diethylamide). These substances may not be produced or sold by anyone. The exception is the federal government itself, which produces them for use free of charge in approved medical research projects.

Chemicals on Schedule II are considered to have a high potential for misuse but also great value in medicine. They may be manufactured privately and sold as prescription drugs. Included in this category are morphine, cocaine, amphetamines, and certain tranquilizers. Cocaine has been used for more than a century as an anaesthetic for the eye during surgery.

Marijuana's Medical Record

Most medicines have more than one effect, and the goal of modern drug companies has been to eliminate side effects, so that drugs have a strong punch in one targeted area and very mild to no effects in others. It may not be possible to remove all the unwanted effects, however, and some medicines are so important that they are used in any case. For example, cortisone is extremely useful for treating inflamed joints, but it also weakens the immune system, making the user more vulnerable to infection. That is a severe side effect. In the same way, smoking marijuana may reduce eye pressure, but it also has a strong effect on the central nervous system. It can cause not only euphoria but also alarming hallucinations, confusion, and short-term memory loss.

The primary active chemical in marijuana is delta-9-tetrahydrocannabinol (THC) — an intoxicant. THC has been isolated and produced synthetically, chiefly for use as an antinausea agent for cancer patients undergoing chemotherapy. Some experiments with THC in eyedrops have been performed on glaucoma patients — with little success. THC

69

pills, likewise, have been of little use in treating glaucoma. But research is still being done in an attempt to isolate compounds in marijuana that might be medically useful, without the intoxicating side effects. So far, the results have been disappointing.

The main disappointment for glaucoma sufferers is that THC does not go to work as reliably or as quickly as marijuana smoke itself. This may have to do with the fact that many other compounds exist in marijuana, and some may boost the power of THC. Then, too, it takes longer for THC to reach the eye if it is introduced to the body as a pill than if it goes directly into the bloodstream from the lungs. The effects of the pill are less consistent. Eye drops containing THC have been tested but without great success. On this basis, Robert Randall argues that smoking marijuana is better than using THC — at least in his case. The courts have supported him thus far.

Medicinal Properties of Marijuana

Randall has won a single exemption from the law so that he may smoke marijuana, but few other patients have benefited. For the most part, doctors do not question the decision on drug classification, and those who wish to give patients Schedule I drugs may do so, but only if they are conducting experimental research. In such cases, the drugs are supplied free by the government, and the doctors who use them must report back to the government on the results of their experiment. Studies concerning marijuana have resulted in some interesting developments concerning some potential medicinal qualities of the drug.

For example, marijuana has been proven useful in preventing the nausea and vomiting common in cancer patients treated with strong chemicals and radiation. It is not clear whether this beneficial effect comes about through a direct impact on the stomach and esophagus or through a general reduction of anxiety. But both marijuana and isolated THC, its active ingredient, have been used to prevent vomiting. According to NIDA's report to Congress in 1984, some patients find these drugs better than any other for this purpose.

On first use, marijuana smoke dilates the breathing passages. Some researchers thought THC might be helpful in treating asthmatic patients who suffer from a sudden constriction of the airways. But prolonged smoking of marijuana actually injures the bronchial passages and may cause breathing problems. In addition, no one has yet found a good way to administer THC to asthmatics. And studies show that THC can have either a helpful or bad effect on asthmatics, an outcome that cannot be predicted in advance. It is therefore not recommended as an antiasthma drug.

Other potential medical uses of marijuana are as a treatment for epileptic convulsions, as a muscle relaxant, as a sedative, as an antibiotic salve, and possibly in the control of some tumors. These uses are not well established and are still under study.

Cancer patient Lynn Pierson petitioned the state of New Mexico to legalize marijuana as a treatment for the side effects of his chemotherapy treatments. His request was granted, but Pierson died months before the new legislation became law.

One problem that complicates research on marijuana is that each batch is slightly different chemically, as is any agricultural product. Furthermore, as marijuana ages, its chemical makeup changes. Thus, standardization is difficult. It is not clear that scientific results from one batch of marijuana can be taken as true for all others. Because of its chemical instability, marijuana would probably have to be kept refrigerated, an expensive feature in any medical product.

The Status of Marijuana Remains Illicit

In 1972, a promarijuana group called the National Organization for the Reform of the Marijuana Laws (NORML) petitioned to have marijuana shifted out of Schedule I into some lower-ranking category. NORML argued that marijuana is not addictive, and that it has an established value in medicine. At that time, it was harder to debate the issue than now because there was so little information. NORML argued that the marijuana weed, which is composed of hundreds of chemicals, has a medicinal value not present in extracts such as THC.

The NORML petition of 1972 marked the first step in a long and tangled legal controversy that has not yet come to an end. At the outset, the government (in the form of the now-extinct Bureau of Narcotics and Dangerous Drugs) rejected the petition without a hearing. NORML sued, saying its request had been thrown out unfairly. An appeals court agreed in 1974 and ordered the government to make a more careful review.

In 1975, the new Drug Enforcement Administration again rejected NORML's petition, but with some care. NORML sued again on the basis that the decision was unscientific and won another victory in 1977. The court required a thorough review of the scientific data. Because there was no action on the case for about two years, NORML sued again in 1979, then again in 1980, resulting in a court order that the entire question of marijuana as medicine be reconsidered by the drug agencies. There have been more petitions, and more orders from the court, but the legal status of marijuana remains unchanged.

More recently, a barrage of lawsuits has brought about one change. In 1986, the government decided to shift THC, the marijuana chemical, from Schedule I to Schedule II, meaning that it may be sold as a prescription drug. Any doctor may give it in cases where cancer patients will benefit. It is no longer totally illicit, but it must be kept in a locked cabinet and closely accounted for, just like morphine.

Although THC is available as medicine, marijuana, whose psychoactive power comes from THC, is not. It is still kept on Schedule I. The members of NORML find this illogical and are pressuring the government to concede that marijuana, if prescribed and administered by a doctor, is as safe as THC. Hearings on this argument began in the late 1980s in Washington at the offices of the Drug Enforcement Administration.

Officials still doubt that there is any merit in NORML's case or in Randall's evidence. DEA's deputy administrator for drug diversion problems, Gene Haislip, gave his personal opinion of Randall's access to federal marijuana in an interview. "It's a scam," he said.

From the enforcement point of view, there are two major reasons for continuing to outlaw the sale of marijuana as a medicine. First is the issue of drug purity and side effects

DEA deputy administrator Gene Haislip remains unconvinced by medical evidence of marijuana's therapeutic value. Despite federal disapproval, several states now allow restricted medical use of marijuana.

discussed earlier. The term *marijuana* covers a great number of chemicals in many different combinations, and the authorities feel it would be irresponsible to license anything so vaguely defined. Haislip, the drug enforcement official responsible for prescription drugs, says the agency is merely acting upon the advice provided by the scientific community. The advice comes from the Food and Drug Administration.

Second, licensing marijuana would create a legal market for it. The existence of a legal market always makes it harder to control the black market, because it complicates the task of enforcement. Legitimate shipments get diverted into the black market; counterfeit versions of the legal drug appear, and the number of people with prescriptions — genuine or not—increases.

The federal government firmly refuses to legalize marijuana as medicine. But a remarkable number of state legislatures has taken this step anyway, goaded into action by NORML and other promarijuana lobbyists. At last count, 32 states had done so, and there have been sporadic moves to legalize home-grown marijuana for use by patients undergoing treatment for cancer. Without federal approval, however, the medical use of smoked marijuana is not likely to grow significantly.

The Other Drugs

Some attention has been given to heroin as a prescription drug, but as yet no change in policy has occurred. There has been a sporadic but unsuccessful effort to license heroin for use by terminal patients suffering extreme pain. In 1984, the U.S. House of Representatives considered a bill (H.R. 5290) that would have made heroin available to cancer patients with "severe, intense, and intractable pain." But it was opposed by the Reagan administration, the American Medical Association, and the International Narcotics Enforcement Officers Association, and it was subsequently defeated.

According to NIDA's report to Congress in 1984, many physicians feel that heroin "is endowed with properties that are especially useful in the treatment of terminal chronic pain." Research continues to show that heroin is more soluble in water and in human tissue than its fellow opiate, morphine, and enters the central nervous system more rapidly. Heroin also appears to be two to three times stronger (by weight) than morphine. According to Dr. Allen Mondzac, a cancer researcher at George Washington University, heroin has another advantage: Its euphoric effect lifts the spirit of patients whose desperate condition often increases their sense of pain. Dr. William Beaver of Georgetown University, who conducted a study comparing heroin and morphine, wrote, "There will be individual patients who respond better to heroin for reasons we do not understand."

Yet some other researchers — including Kathleen Foley and Raymond Houde of the Memorial Sloan-Kettering Cancer Research Center in New York — say there is no significant benefit to using heroin rather than morphine. They suggest that the only advantage of heroin is that smaller amounts are needed to bring the same degree of pain relief as do larger doses of morphine. Federal health officials do not regard this advantage as important enough to merit licensing the drug as a marketable medicine. Dr. Edward Tocus of the Food and Drug Administration, who oversees experimental research in this area, says that there is a better, more powerful painkiller on the market now, the narcotic analgesic Dilaudid. But the advocates of hospital use of heroin say the government allowed the use of this new drug, a more soluble version of morphine, only because it had been criticized for keeping heroin out of doctors' hands. They also say it has not been around long enough for doctors to know whether it compares well with heroin, which has been manufactured since the 1870s.

Heroin is now available for doctors who wish to investigate it, but not for regular use as a painkiller. According to Tocus, applications for heroin research are on the decline.

Studies of a cancer clinic recorded in the *Annals of the New York Academy of Sciences* indicate that doctors tend to err on the side of giving too little, not too much painkiller. Many doctors still fear that patients will become addicted to medicine, a concern that dates from the injudicious use of morphine during the Civil War. This concern may be misplaced in the late 20th century, for the amount of narcotics available on the black market is many times larger than the amount that might be used in hospitals. According to Dr.

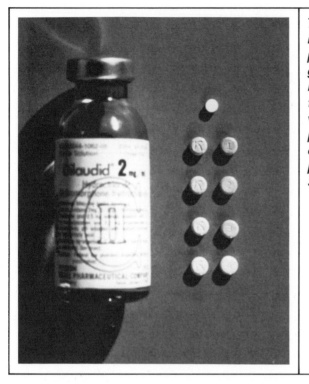

The narcotic Dilaudid is the medication preferred by government officials to heroin for treating terminally ill patients who suffer severe pain. Heroin is currently not a legal painkiller in the United States.

Mondac, the total demand for medical heroin might be around 4% of the volume now sold illegally on the street. Furthermore, there is little evidence to support the fear that the use of painkillers in the hospital increases the risk of addiction.

Doctors in the United States have not been allowed to prescribe heroin for any purpose other than experimental research since 1970, and for all practical purposes, medical use of heroin stopped in this country in the 1920s. But in the United Kingdom, heroin is still used as a painkiller, having never been entirely banned.

According to the National Committee on the Treatment of Intractable Pain (NCTIP), a group in Washington, D.C., British doctors in recent years have begun to use heroin more frequently as a painkiller, and the medical demand for the drug grew from around 57 kilograms in 1974 to 228 kilograms in 1985. Canada also decided to permit doctors to prescribe heroin for cancer patients in 1986.

New bills were introduced in Congress in 1987 to make the use of heroin legal in hospitals. One version (H.R. 1470) was sponsored by Representative Henry Waxman in the House and the other (S 143) by Senator Daniel Inouye in the Senate. These bills are still pending.

There are, of course, those who feel that legalizing the medical use of such drugs as marijuana and heroin would strengthen the case for the legalization of these drugs for recreational purposes. Their opponents would argue that these are two separate issues; legalizing the medicinal use of these drugs would not inevitably result in legal social use. Still others argue that, at least for marijuana, the best possible answer is complete legalization — for both medicinal and recreational purposes. This argument is the subject of Chapter 5.

In his essay On Liberty, *the English philosopher John Stuart Mill defended the right of individuals to live free from governmental regulation, providing they caused no harm to others.*

THE CASE FOR LEGALIZING MARIJUANA USE

The United States stands apart from many nations in its deep respect for the individual. The strong belief in personal freedom appears early in the nation's history.

The Declaration of Independence speaks of every citizen's right to "life, liberty, and the pursuit of happiness." The Constitution and Bill of Rights go further, making specific guarantees. They forbid the government to make unwarranted entry into dwelling places. They forbid seizure of personal property, except when very clear reasons are approved by the courts. They allow every citizen to remain silent in court when accused of a crime. Legal decisions have extended these rights, so that every citizen may feel safe, secure, and sheltered from public view in the privacy of his or her home.

The Right to Privacy

In recent years, Americans have referred to privacy as one of the basic human rights, something to be claimed by anyone, anywhere. United States citizens feel strongly about this and often tell other countries that they must honor their people's

The Declaration of Independence, signed in 1776, guaranteed every citizen's right to "life, liberty, and the pursuit of happiness." Americans have always considered personal freedom a fundamental right.

claims to privacy and personal freedom. Foreign leaders often disagree. They resent what they deem arrogant meddling by the United States. Leaders of the Soviet Union, for example, regard individual privacy as trivial when compared to the needs of the state.

If the United States is to be persuasive in promoting freedom in other parts of the world, it must respect the privacy of its own citizens. Sometimes it is hard to do this because what goes on in people's private lives may seem offensive. But, according to U.S. traditions, there is a strong case to be made against legislating the private behavior of adults, so long as that behavior does not in turn violate the rights of others.

One of the strongest advocates of limited government power in the 19th century was the English philosopher John Stuart Mill. In his famous 1859 essay *On Liberty*, he wrote that governments have no right to direct the private "tastes and pursuits" of their citizens. Adults should be allowed to live as they wish, provided they do not harm others. On this basis, he argued that the state should not outlaw alcohol or opium. To do so would be to substitute the government's tastes and moral judgments for those of the individual, an unjustified violation of personal freedom by the state.

Mill argued that the only reasonable basis for restricting personal habits (such as drinking) was to protect others from injury. Furthermore, he said, protective laws must not be based solely on possible future injuries, but on the evidence that real injuries have occurred in the past. In this way, a soldier's drinking at home should not be illegal, but drinking while on duty should be.

Some people feel that this reasoning should hold also for marijuana. A person who smokes at home is not doing injury. The marijuana user is indulging in a minor pleasure over which that government should have no jurisdiction. It is quite clear from survey data that most people do not become physically dependent on marijuana. The majority use it as others use alcohol — to relax occasionally and to indulge a festive mood. How can a mild intoxicant, taken less than once a day by most users, be seen as a public threat?

Even those who are "hooked," or psychologically dependent upon their habit, should not be penalized by the law. Some people find any compulsive and unproductive behavior disgusting. But that is not a reason for outlawing it. Consider eating. Many people develop compulsive habits about food. They talk about it frequently. They spend many of their waking hours anticipating, planning, obtaining, and consuming food. This may be unattractive. It certainly is not productive. It can be harmful if the "food addict" is overweight. But there are no laws to prevent food addiction. If Congress tried to forbid the eating of ice cream sundaes or cotton candy, many people would be outraged. Others would simply laugh.

The same sort of argument is raised by some people with respect to marijuana. Even compulsive marijuana smoking by an adult is not so offensive that it injures neighbors or requires government intervention. The attempt to use the law to tell people what they may and may not consume at home is an arrogant invasion of personal privacy.

Protecting the Drug User's Physical Health

Sometimes it is said that the law must protect the drug user from himself. The argument takes two forms. One has to do with the damage a drug may do to a person's health and the other with the individual's power of self-control or freedom. First consider the health effects.

By any reasonable standard, marijuana is a mild drug. The experts at NIDA who keep track of medical data report that marijuana is rarely mentioned in death reports (see Chapter 3). And when it is, it is almost always cited as being used with alcohol or another drug. Perhaps there are some people who are allergic to marijuana smoke and who die from shock when exposed to it. There are not many of them. But then there are people who have the same reaction to fish, and no one proposes to outlaw seafood for that reason.

As for overdosing, there is no scientifically valid evidence of anyone dying of an overdose of marijuana smoke. Of course, it is possible to commit suicide by consuming large amounts of marijuana. But it is possible to die by eating too much salt. Salt is not illegal. Aspirin kills by overdose. It is legal. Many people die by drinking too much alcohol, an addictive drug. It too is legal. Why is marijuana considered more dangerous?

What about the damage done by smoking marijuana over a period of many years? A great deal has been written about these "chronic effects" of marijuana use. The strongest theory in this area is the one that compares the smoke from marijuana to that from tobacco. Both have a harmful effect on the bronchial passages. Both contain toxic chemicals. Tar extracted from them causes cancer when painted on the skin of mice. Tobacco smoke is known to cause lung cancer in cigarette smokers, and there is mounting evidence that marijuana smoke can do the same.

Merely to state these facts is to beg a question: Why does evidence on the danger of tobacco argue for a ban on marijuana? Doesn't it argue for a ban on tobacco? Even if we were to make a jump in logic and conclude that the real threat comes not from tobacco but marijuana, we would have to consider that marijuana is smoked in much smaller quantities — not at a rate of 20, 40, or 60 cigarettes a day, as tobacco often is. For this reason, the tobacco data are not relevant for estimating the cancer risk of marijuana.

What of other problems, such as the impact on motivation? As many reviewers have said, it is hard to draw a conclusion from the fact that some marijuana smokers seem to lack energy and are depressed. The trouble is, no one can be certain which comes first: the marijuana or the depression. It may be that depressed adolescents seek out drugs just as much as certain drugs make adolescents depressed. If that is so, then it is difficult to see any cause-and-effect relationship between using marijuana and losing energy. The issue needs more study.

Marijuana does have an effect on memory and motor skills. It is true that heavy use of the drug makes it hard to learn, and this would interfere with the educational process. But heavy use of any psychoactive drug — including the legal ones — is likely to interfere with schoolwork. Marijuana is also likely to slow social and emotional development. The

A satirical look at how legalization of marijuana might affect public places.

sensible response to this threat is not to make marijuana illegal for adults, but to improve the controls that keep children from using any drugs, legal or not.

The other risks of long-term smoking of marijuana, such as injury to the immune and reproductive systems, are not so clear. They may be real, but they are hard to detect, which suggests that even if they are identified, they may not be significant. The evidence supporting the theory that marijuana use damages the brain is even less substantial. In fact, in 1982 the report of the National Academy of Sciences, entitled *Marijuana and Health: Record of Study* found the studies on brain damage caused by marijuana to be "unconvincing." It noted that long-term, heavy users of marijuana are more likely than other people to suffer from mental and behavioral problems, but it was not clear whether the problems were caused by marijuana, or by outside factors having nothing to do with the drug.

One final point needs to be made about the relationship between marijuana and individual physical health. Because under the present system users can only get marijuana from illegal sources, there is no guarantee that what they are getting is pure. Indeed, there have been cases in which a user has smoked what he or she believed was pure marijuana, only to experience hazardous or even fatal effects because dangerous substances, such as the hallucinogen PCP, had been added to the drug. Obviously, the legalization of marijuana would make it subject to governmental regulation and control, and hence, safeguard its purity.

What should be done to deal with all the health risks of marijuana is to make the users aware of the dangers. Education rather than prohibition should be stressed. Once the dangers are publicized, it should be up to the user, rather than the government, to decide whether the risks are too great. After all, mountain climbers live with extreme danger, but they go on climbing mountains. Motorcycle riders die in vast numbers, but this does not stop others from riding. They enjoy the risk. Football injuries cripple dozens of people every year, and may even inflict permanent brain damage on some. But football is legal. Cigarette smoking exposes millions of Americans each year to the dangers of lung cancer and heart disease, but it is not illegal. Why should marijuana be treated differently?

Protecting the User's Mind or Identity

Set aside health effects and consider the subtle issue of protecting a person against the tendency to become a slave to an addiction. This is an issue of psychological health.

In this case, it is said that drugs are more dangerous than other risky pursuits because they take over the mind. A regular user loses self-control. The addiction takes over and the person becomes a prisoner of the chemical. Using this logic, some argue that society has a duty to intervene and "liberate" the addict from the drug. The way to do this, it is said, is to make habit-forming drugs illegal and nearly impossible to get. This reduces the risk that people will enslave themselves.

The idea is interesting, but is it valid? First, as many researchers have found, only about 5 to 10% of drug users are intensely compulsive, daily users. The most extreme estimates put the number of addicts at no more than 20 to 25% of users. This means that at least 75 to 80% of the people who use drugs are not addicted to them.

Does it make sense to restrict the freedom of all the people who want to smoke marijuana to protect the minority who become compulsive? Clearly the public does not care to do this with regard to alcohol, a drug that appears to be more addictive than marijuana. It prefers to tolerate some misuse of this drug so that most users may enjoy it in moderation. This is the way the law usually works when there is a big demand for a product that is dangerous for a small percentage of buyers. Often, the law deals with this problem by requiring products to be labeled so that every user will be aware of the dangers. This is done with medical drugs, many of which may be deadly for some patients.

Consider gambling as another example. Some people lose self-control in a gambling casino. They bet without constraint until all their money is gone. These compulsive gamblers make up a small percentage of all those who use the casino. But the government does not totally prohibit gambling in order to protect this minority. In terms of its potency, marijuana is more like Bingo than blackjack. Imagine a crusade to outlaw Bingo parlors in order to save people from enslavement!

According to another theory mentioned earlier, marijuana may be a "stepping-stone" or "gateway" on the path to

Gamblers place their bets at a casino in Atlantic City. Gambling, which can become a compulsive habit, is legal for adults in some states; many people believe marijuana should be similarly permitted.

more powerful drugs. Stopping the progress of the drug user by making marijuana scarce, it is argued, will make it likely that fewer people will go on to more serious drugs such as cocaine and heroin. True, studies have shown that most heroin and cocaine users had prior experiences with marijuana. But they had also used tobacco and alcohol. No one uses this fact to argue for prohibition of alcohol.

Furthermore, it has not been established conclusively that the use of marijuana encourages people to go on to other drugs. As the National Academy of Sciences concluded in its definitive 1982 study: "There is no evidence to support the belief that the use of one drug will inevitably lead to use of any other drug. In other words, persons at the top of the ladder of drug use will have used all substances at lower levels, including marijuana. However, those at lower rungs may stay there and not move to higher rungs of the ladder."

In short, marijuana must be judged on its own faults, not on the faults of other drugs.

As for the people who become addicted to marijuana, the best thing to do is to offer them treatment, as is done for alcoholics. It does not make sense to call them criminals and punish them. It makes even less sense to punish moderate or infrequent users.

Protecting Society from Marijuana

One argument made against the legalization of marijuana is that it damages not only the user but innocent bystanders. This argument, like the one about protecting the user, has two parts. The first deals with physical injury and the second with spiritual health.

The main physical threat to society is that users under the influence of a drug will crash a car or airplane, or lose control in some way and do harm. People who have recently smoked marijuana do show signs of clumsiness and disorientation. They should not operate machinery in this condition. One study estimates that alcohol plays a part in 55% of all fatal highway crashes. Marijuana may present similar risks, but at present there are no reliable data on its importance in accidents.

According to John Stuart Mill's writings, the government should try to control only the aspects of drug use that injure society. In this vein, it makes sense to have laws against driving under the influence of marijuana similar to those governing driving under the influence of alcohol. In other words, driving while on marijuana should be outlawed but not the use of marijuana itself.

Some people believe that marijuana threatens society in a more insidious way. They argue that it drains workers' energy and makes them less productive. This in turn lowers the vitality of the economy, depressing the overall quality of life. In addition, drug use — including marijuana smoking — is seen as a plague on society that must be isolated. This disease theory holds that legalizing marijuana would make it more widely available and that this would tend to increase its use as well as the use of all kinds of drugs. One of the detriments of tolerating drug use, according to this theory, is that it encourages the use of more and different drugs.

The National Institute on Drug Abuse's 1984 report to Congress cited no evidence to support the idea that drug use is hurting economic productivity. It said: "The fact is, very little is known about the complex relationship which undoubtedly exists between drug abuse, worker performance, and productivity, or the lack thereof. . . . Simply put, the number of unanswered questions currently far outnumbers the available answers."

Nor is there any strong evidence that legalizing marijuana would increase use of the drug. In fact, there is some evidence suggesting that drug use under a relaxed legal system might not increase at all. Many states have removed the penalties for marijuana possession that were on the books in the 1950s and 1960s. The change occurred during a reform movement that swept the nation in the mid 1970s (see Chapter 1). Yet in spite of the less stringent laws, studies show that the use of marijuana in the affected states has, after an initial increase, declined. Although marijuana became easier to use (from a legal standpoint), it also became less popular.

The Failure of Prohibition

Examining the U.S. policy on marijuana on the basis of performance, one must judge it a miserable failure. The number of people who have smoked the drug at least once has grown from an uncounted few in the 1950s, when some of the strictest antimarijuana laws were imposed, to nearly 50 million today. During this period the federal government has made steadily increasing efforts to stop its production and importation, and seizures of marijuana in the ports has grown steadily. Elaborate and costly international police campaigns have been launched, and the number of drug arrests in the United States has increased. The federal budget for drug enforcement reflected in several agencies has gone above $1 billion a year. And yet the illegal trade in marijuana continues. Supplies are so plentiful that the price has actually come down.

The response has been to redouble police efforts and hope that things will change. The result is that more money is spent on a failed policy, creating an ever-growing army of drug enforcers dedicated to keeping the policy alive. The illegal market for marijuana grows even faster than the police force, however, because the drug users are willing to pay more to get what they want than taxpayers are willing to pay to stop it. The drug police enjoy their work and are not going to quit. And why should they, as long as their salaries are paid? The admission that the marijuana laws have failed will have to come from someone else—not from the police.

The attempt to outlaw marijuana is failing for much the same reason that the attempt to outlaw alcohol failed in the 1920s. The public is not uniformly opposed to it. In fact, a large number of people think that marijuana use is acceptable, and about 18 million use it at least once a month. They like the drug so much that they will break the law to get it, as well as pay the grossly inflated prices charged for it on the black market.

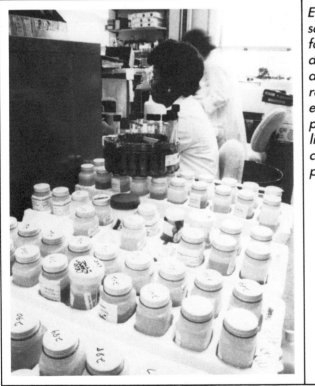

Employees' urine samples await testing for the presence of drugs. The Reagan administration recommends random employee drug testing programs, which civil liberties groups consider a violation of privacy.

Marijuana is a common weed, easier to produce than the bathtub gin of the Prohibition years. It is not surprising that thousands of "dealers" have been drawn into the marijuana business. Despite the great risks they face, including bullying by other dealers and the threat of arrest, they are attracted by the profits. The law cannot change the economics of this market because it operates outside the law. All the police can do is to make it risky to get into the marijuana business. This is supposed to drive out the less courageous dealers, reduce the amount of marijuana available, and inflate prices. But even by this measure, the police effort has failed. As mentioned earlier, the price of marijuana is declining.

There are several ways in which the policy on marijuana imposes a burden on society. The obvious one is the cost of supporting the federal enforcement effort. Aside from this, there is a hard-to-measure but significant impact on society because the law creates a huge criminal class. It includes not just dealers who are out for profit but a much larger group of users. Consider three major penalties for having such a large criminal class.

First, the marijuana laws damage the lives of individual drug users by making them social outcasts. Part of the reason many states changed local marijuana laws to make possession of the drug a minor offense during the 1970s was that citizens were upset by the number of young people being classified as criminals. But the federal law has not changed. This leads to a dangerous situation, for no society can be sure of its stability if a large group of citizens is cast beyond the pale and denied the rights of law-abiding people.

Second, the presence of a large and well-to-do criminal class has a strong corrupting effect on public institutions. Faced with what seems an impossible task, the police may begin to use extreme measures. They may resort increasingly to wiretaps and other forms of spying. Paramilitary operations are mounted in peaceful cities. Police begin to act like dealers themselves in order to make arrests. For example, in one city the drug police have adopted a tactic known as "sell and bust," in which they set up drug shops and, after encouraging a brisk trade in an illegal drug, they jail their customers. At the same time, the federal government is trying to have companies test employees to find out whether they have been using drugs. This is another restriction of citizens' rights, done in the name of enforcing the drug laws.

At the other extreme, some officials have become so overwhelmed by the task at hand that they have ceased to care. Some may even collaborate with the drug dealers. The temptation to do this is strong, especially if the law seems arbitrary, as in the case of marijuana. Selling marijuana is a big business, and plenty of money is available for officials who are willing to cooperate with the black market. Corruption always exists where black markets are found. The bigger the market, the greater the likelihood of corruption.

Third, the existence of a large criminal class has a subtle but destructive effect on the public's regard for law and government. Widespread contempt for the law among marijuana users breeds disrespect for other forms of authority. And the obvious inability of the government to enforce the law breeds a general cynicism, even among nonusers. It causes people to wonder if government policy on other issues should be taken seriously. Citizens may suspect that official policy may be a "bluff" in other cases, too. Governments need the support and the faith of citizens in order to be effective.

Some Benefits of Legalizing Marijuana

By lifting the ban on marijuana use and treating it like other drugs such as tobacco and alcohol, the nation would gain immediate and long-term benefits. This change in the law would greatly improve the quality of life for many people. Victims of glaucoma and those needing antinausea treatment, for example, would find marijuana easily available. If the medical advantages that are claimed for marijuana are real, many more patients would benefit. Research, which has been slowed in the past by the government's reluctance to grant exemptions to the marijuana laws, would be easier to conduct. The cloud of suspicion would disappear, and doctors could get on with investigating marijuana's medical uses without fear of controversy. It might become possible to discuss the dangers of marijuana use without getting caught up in a policy debate.

Meanwhile, the black market would disappear overnight. Some arrangement would be made to license the production

A bird's-eye view of New York City's Washington Square Park, for many years a haven for marijuana dealers. Supporters of legalization stress that if legislation permitting the drug were passed, the formidable marijuana black market would disappear virtually overnight.

of marijuana cigarettes. Thousands of dealers would be put out of business, and a secret part of the economy would come into the open. It is difficult to say whether this change would reduce crime because criminals would probably continue to sell other drugs. But it would have an impact on the amount of money flowing through criminal channels, and this might weaken organized crime.

Lastly, the federal budget would benefit in two ways. Federal revenues would increase, because marijuana cigarettes would be taxed at the point of sale. The companies that make the cigarettes would also pay income taxes, adding to the federal coffers. Second, there would be a reduction in the amount spent on law enforcement efforts to apprehend and prosecute users and sellers of marijuana. The drug enforcement authorities might reduce their budget requests, or, more likely, focus more intensely on hard drugs and violent crimes. The courts would be relieved of hearing some drug cases, as well.

The most important gain would be in the quality of government. The sorts of temptations and opportunities that lead to corruption would be significantly minimized. The illogical pattern of law enforcement, which now treats marijuana as more dangerous than alcohol, would end. It would set more achievable goals for law enforcement, and this would lend strength and credibility to the government.

A candlelight demonstration against drug use was held in New York City in 1986. Public opinion has shifted away from legalization and is in fact calling for tougher drug laws and enforcement instead.

CHAPTER 6

THE CASE FOR PROHIBITING MARIJUANA USE

Laws are merely tools for carrying out what the public wants, and every law is born of human desires. Take away this context, and almost any law will begin to seem dull and arbitrary. So it is with the prohibition of marijuana. It is important in considering the legal issues in drug control not to become distracted by technicalities. The larger social purpose must be kept in mind. The chief federal law on marijuana is called the Comprehensive Drug Abuse Prevention and Control Act, also known as the Controlled Substances Act. Passed by Congress in 1970, it reorganized federal policy, including the Marijuana Tax Act of 1937, into a new strategy to combat drug addiction. This was the most recent time that the nation considered the subject of drugs in its entirety, and it is significant that Congress made no move to relax the policy on marijuana. In fact, the 1970 law strengthened the penalties. There were two major national reviews of policy after that, a complete study of the marijuana issue by a presidential "blue ribbon" panel of experts (National Commission on Marijuana and Drug Abuse, 1973) and a report, entitled *Drug Use in America: Problem in Perspective*, written for all state governors (Governor's Conference Report, 1977). None of them recommended making marijuana legal or even restricted, as alcohol is. National leaders have made no move to legalize marijuana since then.

The best way to question public support for a law is to ask for a vote on it. That is what happened in the case of Prohibition in 1933. If a law fails to win support — as ultimately happened with Prohibition — then it dies. The issue is settled. But those who wish to get rid of the marijuana laws have not been successful.

The reason the federal government has not changed its policy on marijuana is that most citizens do not want it to change. Nothing would prevent Congress from ending the prohibition on marijuana, if there were any popular support

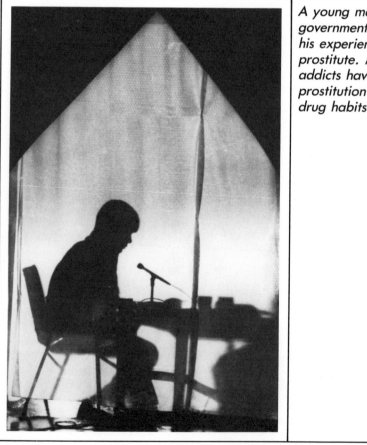

A young man tells government officials of his experiences as a child prostitute. Many young addicts have turned to prostitution to support drug habits.

for ending it. But in the nearly two decades since the passage of the comprehensive drug law, Congress has been relatively content with the results. Not only has there been no repeal, but there has been no significant agitation for repeal. This suggests that the public is satisfied with the way the law works. Most people do not see marijuana as an issue in itself but as part of the larger problem of drug addiction. Citizens support the law because they understand that it is part of a broad strategy to keep the use of all drugs under control. They realize that to say "yes" to marijuana is to give legitimacy to other drugs, and that inevitably this will lead to the expanded use of other dangerous substances.

Privacy and the Law

The right to personal privacy has a strong traditional basis in the United States. But it has never been understood to include the freedom to use drugs. Drug abuse is not one of the "natural rights" the founding fathers aimed to protect. The right to privacy — which they did mean to protect — does not include the right to buy marijuana.

The privacy standard does not apply because drug addiction is not a private matter. It is a burden for those who live with it and a trial for their families. Addicts strain the medical system, using resources that would be better spent on the victims of natural disease. Their problems are a burden to state and federal budgets, for taxpayers must finance drug treatment programs. Addiction takes a toll on the economy, draining away productivity and shortening lives. Addiction tends to proliferate, moving from one neighborhood to another, like a disease. The drug user influences many lives beyond his or her own immediate world, often for the worse.

Before looking at the damage done by drug use, consider another controversial situation in which Constitutional rights play a part — child pornography. It, too, involves a clash between personal rights and the claims of society. On one hand, citizens are entitled to buy and read whatever they wish. The right to free speech is guaranteed by the Constitution. But, on the other hand, one cannot produce such pornography without violating the rights of children. (Children are too young to give consent knowingly.) In this case, the rights of children are more important than those of free speech.

The same rule applies to marijuana. Society has an overriding interest in stopping the spread of drug abuse. It particularly wishes to protect children from this self-destructive way of life. Among the drugs of concern are heroin, cocaine, and marijuana. To be effective in stopping the spread of addiction, controls must be imposed on all these drugs. Thus, the minority who use marijuana lose some of their freedom to do what they wish in private. But society gains a great deal more; it obtains relief from drug addiction.

Marijuana and Personal Health

Expert reports on marijuana are carefully written because the subject is so controversial. Scientists do not like to step far beyond the proven facts in giving a conclusion, and in regard to drugs, they are more than usually cautious. Reports often say that a damaging health effect is "not proven" even though some evidence of injury is in hand. What this means is that although the evidence may be true, it is not strong enough to persuade everyone that the effect is real. Often reports end by saying, "more study is needed," indicating that the experts decline to issue a verdict, similar to a hung jury. They refuse to judge marijuana "guilty" or "not guilty" without more evidence.

Not everyone can afford to be neutral. Although it is unwise to reach broad conclusions when experts disagree, people must reach decisions in their own lives about risks such as those associated with drugs, even when the experts are undecided. Public health officials also must set policy. So it makes sense to study the evidence and act on it, even if it is not possible to know the final "truth."

There may be no "proof" that smoking marijuana causes lung cancer, but there is evidence that it damages the lining of the bronchial passages in the same way that smoking cigarettes does. It is well known — even "proven" by scientific standards — that cigarette smoke causes cancer and other diseases. There is, in addition, evidence that tar from marijuana smoke stimulates cancer in mice. It is more powerful than tobacco smoke in this regard. For this reason, it is not just a suspicion that marijuana smoke can cause cancer, but a reasonable theory. No one knows how much smoking it takes to start a tumor, but it is reasonable to assume that the more one smokes, the greater the risk.

Evidence suggests, but has not proven, that heavy use of marijuana may damage health in several other ways. Some of this information comes from laboratory animals, whose metabolism is different from humans'. The effects include

•Short-term stress on the heart and circulatory system.

•Short-term confusion of memory, loss of motor skills, and distortion of perception.

•Changes in brain wave patterns and trouble in learning, months after heavy use of marijuana is stopped.

•Potential disruption of male and female reproductive systems.

•Potential suppression of the immune system.

•Possible "addiction," in the sense of physical and psychological dependence.

Any drug that produces these changes in the body cannot be considered mild. The fact that marijuana does not regularly kill people does not make it safe. Its worst effects may be slow-acting and insidious. The cumulative injuries sustained by a regular marijuana user may well prove worse than those experienced by a tobacco smoker. It took several decades to establish that cigarette smoking can be lethal; it may take as long to settle some of the health questions about marijuana. In addition the ready availability of tobacco does not argue for putting another dangerous drug on the market. On the contrary, it suggests that we now may have an opportunity to learn from mistakes made in the past. Using the knowledge gained over the years from tobacco, public health officials may be able to prevent a new epidemic of self-induced cancer, heart disease, and psychological problems.

Some say the individual should be allowed to decide whether or not to accept the health risks of smoking marijuana. The government has no business meddling in this private matter, just as it has no right to outlaw skiing, football, or mountain climbing — all of which are dangerous. But there is an important difference between these activities and smoking marijuana. The drug has an effect on perception. Heavy smokers often use marijuana in a compulsive way and seem to become dependent on it — physically dependent, some researchers say. Long-term use has also been associated with apathetic or passive behavior. This suggests that people who use it may not be able to exercise "adult judgment" in weighing the risks and benefits of continued, prolonged use. In some cases, society must provide the sober judgment the user may no longer possess. It is not enough just to attach a warning label.

Marijuana and Public Health

The clearest threat marijuana poses to the nonuser is through its power to intoxicate drivers of cars, planes, buses, and other types of machinery essential to our society. Automobile, train, and plane accidents caused by drug-affected drivers are obvious hazards to society. There are, once again, no reliable data on this potentially significant issue. But stories about individual cases are easy to find. One of the worst rail tragedies in United States history occurred on January 4, 1987

Firefighters climb onto a derailed Amtrak train that had collided with a Conrail train in January 1987. Traces of marijuana were found in the blood of the Conrail engineers responsible for the crash.

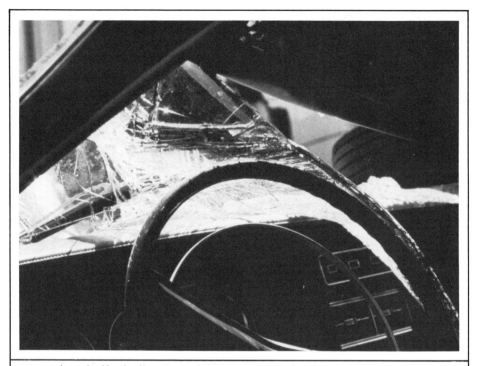

More than half of all automobile accidents, the leading cause of teenage fatalities, are due to alcohol. Many believe that legalizing marijuana would pave the way for even more road accidents and deaths.

when an Amtrak passenger train collided with a Conrail train just north of Washington, D.C. Sixteen passengers were killed and 175 injured. Nearly an entire train was destroyed. After the accident, it was discovered that several of the engineers on the Conrail train had traces of marijuana in their system.

The National Academy of Sciences has concluded (*Marijuana and Health*, 1982) that people who volunteered to take a computerized simulated-driving test after smoking marijuana exhibited diminished skills after "moderately intoxicating doses of marijuana." The same results were obtained using cars on a closed driving course. But researchers have had trouble studying the role marijuana intoxication has played in actual car accidents. One problem is that the drug is hard to detect in the body, although it may impair driving for as long as eight hours after the obvious effects wear off.

This fact has implications for the law. It means that it would be difficult to prove intoxication by marijuana, making it hard to enforce a ban on drugged driving. This is another reason for keeping a general prohibition on marijuana use, rather than a limited ban on smoking-and-driving.

A subtle but extremely important threat to public health is the danger that young people may become regular users of marijuana. The theory that this "soft" drug paves the way like a stepping stone to "hard" drugs is debated among researchers. But anyone who has had experience with long-term, dedicated marijuana smokers has seen the damage it does to their lives, whether or not it ends in hard-core addiction. NIDA's 1984 report to Congress describes the pattern well.

The trouble begins, the report says, when a young person is offered some marijuana at a party. This may happen several times, and gradually the young person's circle of friends consists more and more exclusively of drug users. As marijuana smoking becomes more frequent, the person begins to get involved in buying and selling. "The youth has discovered a way to supplement his income while maintaining his own supply of the drug." This usually results in an acquaintance with a professional dealer, who may offer a chance to try another drug, such as cocaine, as a reward for being a good customer. As NIDA's report concludes, this is not remarkably different from the way things work in the regular business world, except that the consequences for everyone involved are grave indeed.

It is precisely because adolescents are more vulnerable than adults that they are the primary target of the drug trade. They are more susceptible to the psychological effects of marijuana, and they are less able to understand the risks. They are the weak point at which this social disease finds entry. It is not just the individual, but whole communities who are put at risk. "The scenario," says NIDA, "has occurred time and again, throughout the United States, in the urban ghetto and in the tree-lined streets of practically every suburban neighborhood in our country." Drug use is a threat to public health, most intensely threatening to young people. It can be resisted only by an organized strategy of control, such as the law provides.

The Problems of Prohibition

According to social surveys, about 18 million people regularly use marijuana in the United States. Some observers say this means that the laws have failed. But this is not the right conclusion to draw from the numbers. If marijuana is as seductive as alcohol — and many users say it is better — then we should compare the number of marijuana smokers with alcohol drinkers to get a clear picture of how well the law works.

A common estimate is that there are 100 million drinkers in the United States. Ten million of them are "problem drinkers" and 25 million are "potential problem drinkers." This is what the legal status of alcohol has bestowed on society. There is every reason to expect that if marijuana were made legal, the number of marijuana addicts would eventually begin to compete with the number of alcoholics.

Whatever may have been wrong with the alcohol Prohibition of the 1920s, it cannot be blamed for increasing the rate of alcoholism. On the contrary, objective reviewers have found that the number of people with alcohol-related diseases declined sharply during this time (see Chapter 3). It was the relaxation of controls in 1933 that made public drinking acceptable again, and today we are paying the price in auto accidents, stress on the medical system, and personal suffering. That there are 18 million marijuana users today does not show that the existing law has failed so much as it shows what could happen if controls were removed entirely.

That the existing law is not perfect does not mean it should be discarded. Imperfect controls on drug addiction are better than no controls. To argue that prohibition is useless because it is hard to enforce is to surrender to defeatism. It is akin to saying that it is much better to surrender to a hostile invading force than to resist because the enemy has more troops.

Sometimes the laws against drug abuse are blamed for making criminals of marijuana smokers or for creating a black market. This kind of thinking represents a mistake in assigning cause and effect. Those who choose to violate the law do so of their own will — laws do not make people act one way or another. They merely express codes of conduct endorsed by the majority.

Vice-President George Bush looks on as schoolchildren are taught to "say no to drugs." Education and public awareness are crucial weapons in the nationwide battle against drug abuse.

The "Benefits" of Legalizing Marijuana

One of the arguments made by those who favor legalization is that by abolishing the law on marijuana, drug-related crime will decrease or disappear. This is wishful thinking. The criminals who run the illegal organizations supplying millions of tons of contraband to American drug users each year are tough. They are not about to give up. On the contrary, if marijuana were removed from the illicit channels dealers control they would work even harder to peddle the drugs that have not been made legal. They would do everything in their power to boost the market for cocaine and heroin — for these would become the new "in" drugs for those who want to live dangerously.

As far as the medical use of marijuana is concerned, the case of Robert Randall, the glaucoma patient, is exceptional. Ophthalmologists have not petitioned the government in significant numbers to use marijuana. Randall himself relies more heavily on other glaucoma medicines, suggesting that marijuana may be only a minor part of his therapy.

Science has not established that smoking marijuana is preferable to using THC, the active chemical in marijuana, in pill form. Research on this issue is still underway. Meanwhile, physicians who wish to test marijuana against THC for effectiveness in treating glaucoma, nausea, or any other ailment are free to do so. They need only seek approval from the Food and Drug Administration. If and when the scientific community decides that the marijuana plant has a place in medicine, it will be approved for use. Until then it must be treated as an experimental substance.

The same rule applies to heroin. Although research has found it to be a more potent painkiller by weight than morphine (it is a modified version of morphine), no one argues that a dose of heroin is more potent than a double dose of morphine. To achieve a heroinlike potency, the doctor needs only to increase the amount of morphine used. The economic advantage of using heroin rather than morphine is negligible, and there appears to be no medical advantage to using heroin in place of morphine in the hospital.

One advantage of legalizing marijuana, it is argued, is that it will provide income for the federal government. This is another promise that might never pan out. Although taxes collected on marijuana sales might be large, the gain must be weighed against the probable increase in compulsive drug use and drug-related accidents. Recall that the cost to the economy of alcohol abuse is now twice that of drug abuse. If the public responded to legal marijuana in the same way it did to the fall of Prohibition in 1933, the increase in tax revenue probably would not be equal to the economic losses. Severe marijuana intoxication might become commonplace. Treatment programs might have to expand.

In any case, for humane and ethical reasons alike, the government should not sell out the health of its citizens just to increase its income. It has a responsibility to prevent drug use from growing even if it costs the Treasury more.

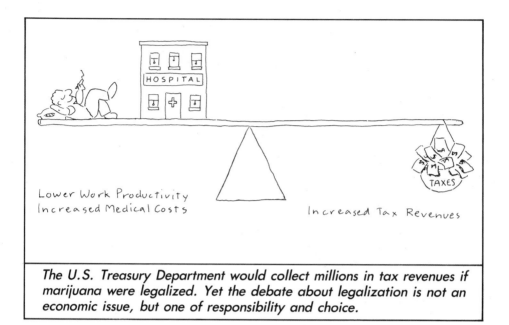

The U.S. Treasury Department would collect millions in tax revenues if marijuana were legalized. Yet the debate about legalization is not an economic issue, but one of responsibility and choice.

Finally, it is perverse to state that the government or the police would gain credibility if marijuana were legalized. If official failure to enforce a statute breeds noncompliance and cynicism among the public, the antidote for this would be to enforce that statute more strenuously, not to abandon it. The reaction in the mid-1980s to drunken driving is a good illustration of this point. When penalties meted out to those convicted of driving while under the influence of alcohol, even when they had injured or killed another while doing so, were lax, there was a widespread public perception that getting behind the wheel of a car after having had too much to drink was no big deal. When, however, after a groundswell of public protest against drunken driving, law enforcement officials began to stiffen penalties for this offense, and rigorously to impose those penalties, the rate of drunken driving began to fall. So too, one might argue, would it be with consistent enforcement of sanctions against the use of marijuana. If the public perceived that the police took the prohibition of this drug seriously, they would likely follow suit. As matters now stand, it is almost as if public nonchalance about the illegality of marijuana follows on official indifference, and not vice versa.

It is important to keep in mind that the prohibition of marijuana is part of a strategy designed to limit the availability of all dangerous drugs. Walking away from the challenge to this strategy will not make it disappear. Retreating from the hard work that is necessary to enforce the marijuana laws will not make it any easier to enforce the laws against cocaine, heroin, and other destructive drugs. On the contrary, the retreat on marijuana would stand as a precedent. Those who want to legalize other drugs would point to the decision and ask, "Why not cocaine, too?" They would do this in exactly the way that they now point to alcohol and say, "Why not marijuana?" In fact, these would be very difficult questions to answer if marijuana were made legal.

The prudent course, for strategic reasons and for public welfare, is to stand firm. The addictive substances that are already available and legal — alcohol and tobacco — do quite enough damage as it is. There is no reason to add another to the list.

APPENDIX

State Agencies
for the Prevention and Treatment
of Drug Abuse

ALABAMA
Department of Mental Health
Division of Mental Illness and
    Substance Abuse Community
    Programs
200 Interstate Park Drive
P.O. Box 3710
Montgomery, AL 36193
(205) 271-9253

ALASKA
Department of Health and Social
    Services
Office of Alcoholism and Drug
    Abuse
Pouch H-05-F
Juneau, AK 99811
(907) 586-6201

ARIZONA
Department of Health Services
Division of Behavioral Health
    Services
Bureau of Community Services
Alcohol Abuse and Alcoholism
    Section
2500 East Van Buren
Phoenix, AZ 85008
(602) 255-1238

Department of Health Services
Division of Behavioral Health
    Services
Bureau of Community Services
Drug Abuse Section
2500 East Van Buren
Phoenix, AZ 85008
(602) 255-1240

ARKANSAS
Department of Human Services
Office of Alcohol and Drug Abuse
    Prevention
1515 West 7th Avenue
Suite 310
Little Rock, AR 72202
(501) 371-2603

CALIFORNIA
Department of Alcohol and Drug
    Abuse
111 Capitol Mall
Sacramento, CA 95814
(916) 445-1940

COLORADO
Department of Health
Alcohol and Drug Abuse Division
4210 East 11th Avenue
Denver, CO 80220
(303) 320-6137

CONNECTICUT
Alcohol and Drug Abuse
    Commission
999 Asylum Avenue
3rd Floor
Hartford, CT 06105
(203) 566-4145

DELAWARE
Division of Mental Health
Bureau of Alcoholism and Drug
    Abuse
1901 North Dupont Highway
Newcastle, DE 19720
(302) 421-6101

DISTRICT OF COLUMBIA
Department of Human Services
Office of Health Planning and
 Development
601 Indiana Avenue, NW
Suite 500
Washington, D.C. 20004
(202) 724-5641

FLORIDA
Department of Health and
 Rehabilitative Services
Alcoholic Rehabilitation Program
1317 Winewood Boulevard
Room 187A
Tallahassee, FL 32301
(904) 488-0396

Department of Health and
 Rehabilitative Services
Drug Abuse Program
1317 Winewood Boulevard
Building 6, Room 155
Tallahassee, FL 32301
(904) 488-0900

GEORGIA
Department of Human Resources
Division of Mental Health and
 Mental Retardation
Alcohol and Drug Section
618 Ponce De Leon Avenue, NE
Atlanta, GA 30365-2101
(404) 894-4785

HAWAII
Department of Health
Mental Health Division
Alcohol and Drug Abuse Branch
1250 Punch Bowl Street
P.O. Box 3378
Honolulu, HI 96801
(808) 548-4280

IDAHO
Department of Health and Welfare
Bureau of Preventive Medicine
Substance Abuse Section
450 West State
Boise, ID 83720
(208) 334-4368

ILLINOIS
Department of Mental Health and
 Developmental Disabilities
Division of Alcoholism
160 North La Salle Street
Room 1500
Chicago, IL 60601
(312) 793-2907

Illinois Dangerous Drugs
 Commission
300 North State Street
Suite 1500
Chicago, IL 60610
(312) 822-9860

INDIANA
Department of Mental Health
Division of Addiction Services
429 North Pennsylvania Street
Indianapolis, IN 46204
(317) 232-7816

IOWA
Department of Substance Abuse
505 5th Avenue
Insurance Exchange Building
Suite 202
Des Moines, IA 50319
(515) 281-3641

KANSAS
Department of Social Rehabilitation
Alcohol and Drug Abuse Services
2700 West 6th Street
Biddle Building
Topeka, KS 66606
(913) 296-3925

KENTUCKY
Cabinet for Human Resources
Department of Health Services
Substance Abuse Branch
275 East Main Street
Frankfort, KY 40601
(502) 564-2880

LOUISIANA
Department of Health and Human
   Resources
Office of Mental Health and
   Substance Abuse
655 North 5th Street
P.O. Box 4049
Baton Rouge, LA 70821
(504) 342-2565

MAINE
Department of Human Services
Office of Alcoholism and Drug
   Abuse Prevention
Bureau of Rehabilitation
32 Winthrop Street
Augusta, ME 04330
(207) 289-2781

MARYLAND
Alcoholism Control Administration
201 West Preston Street
Fourth Floor
Baltimore, MD 21201
(301) 383-2977

State Health Department
Drug Abuse Administration
201 West Preston Street
Baltimore, MD 21201
(301) 383-3312

MASSACHUSETTS
Department of Public Health
Division of Alcoholism
755 Boylston Street
Sixth Floor
Boston, MA 02116
(617) 727-1960

Department of Public Health
Division of Drug Rehabilitation
600 Washington Street
Boston, MA 02114
(617) 727-8617

MICHIGAN
Department of Public Health
Office of Substance Abuse Services
3500 North Logan Street
P.O. Box 30035
Lansing, MI 48909
(517) 373-8603

MINNESOTA
Department of Public Welfare
Chemical Dependency Program
   Division
Centennial Building
658 Cedar Street
4th Floor
Saint Paul, MN 55155
(612) 296-4614

MISSISSIPPI
Department of Mental Health
Division of Alcohol and Drug Abuse
1102 Robert E. Lee Building
Jackson, MS 39201
(601) 359-1297

MISSOURI
Department of Mental Health
Division of Alcoholism and Drug
   Abuse
2002 Missouri Boulevard
P.O. Box 687
Jefferson City, MO 65102
(314) 751-4942

MONTANA
Department of Institutions
Alcohol and Drug Abuse Division
1539 11th Avenue
Helena, MT 59620
(406) 449-2827

NEBRASKA
Department of Public Institutions
Division of Alcoholism and Drug
Abuse
801 West Van Dorn Street
P.O. Box 94728
Lincoln, NB 68509
(402) 471-2851, Ext. 415

NEVADA
Department of Human Resources
Bureau of Alcohol and Drug Abuse
505 East King Street
Carson City, NV 89710
(702) 885-4790

NEW HAMPSHIRE
Department of Health and Welfare
Office of Alcohol and Drug Abuse
  Prevention
Hazen Drive
Health and Welfare Building
Concord, NH 03301
(603) 271-4627

NEW JERSEY
Department of Health
Division of Alcoholism
129 East Hanover Street CN 362
Trenton, NJ 08625
(609) 292-8949

Department of Health
Division of Narcotic and Drug
  Abuse Control
129 East Hanover Street CN 362
Trenton, NJ 08625
(609) 292-8949

NEW MEXICO
Health and Environment Department
Behavioral Services Division
Substance Abuse Bureau
725 Saint Michaels Drive
P.O. Box 968
Santa Fe, NM 87503
(505) 984-0020, Ext. 304

NEW YORK
Division of Alcoholism and Alcohol
  Abuse
194 Washington Avenue
Albany, NY 12210
(518) 474-5417

Division of Substance Abuse
  Services
Executive Park South
Box 8200
Albany, NY 12203
(518) 457-7629

NORTH CAROLINA
Department of Human Resources
Division of Mental Health, Mental
  Retardation and Substance Abuse
  Services
Alcohol and Drug Abuse Services
325 North Salisbury Street
Albemarle Building
Raleigh, NC 27611
(919) 733-4670

NORTH DAKOTA
Department of Human Services
Division of Alcoholism and Drug
  Abuse
State Capitol Building
Bismarck, ND 58505
(701) 224-2767

OHIO
Department of Health
Division of Alcoholism
246 North High Street
P.O. Box 118
Columbus, OH 43216
(614) 466-3543

Department of Mental Health
Bureau of Drug Abuse
65 South Front Street
Columbus, OH 43215
(614) 466-9023

OKLAHOMA
Department of Mental Health
Alcohol and Drug Programs
4545 North Lincoln Boulevard
Suite 100 East Terrace
P.O. Box 53277
Oklahoma City, OK 73152
(405) 521-0044

OREGON
Department of Human Resources
Mental Health Division
Office of Programs for Alcohol and
Drug Problems
2575 Bittern Street, NE
Salem, OR 97310
(503) 378-2163

PENNSYLVANIA
Department of Health
Office of Drug and Alcohol
Programs
Commonwealth and Forster Avenues
Health and Welfare Building
P.O. Box 90
Harrisburg, PA 17108
(717) 787-9857

RHODE ISLAND
Department of Mental Health,
Mental Retardation and Hospitals
Division of Substance Abuse
Substance Abuse Administration
Building
Cranston, RI 02920
(401) 464-2091

SOUTH CAROLINA
Commission on Alcohol and Drug
Abuse
3700 Forest Drive
Columbia, SC 29204
(803) 758-2521

SOUTH DAKOTA
Department of Health
Division of Alcohol and Drug Abuse
523 East Capitol, Joe Foss Building
Pierre, SD 57501
(605) 773-4806

TENNESSEE
Department of Mental Health and
Mental Retardation
Alcohol and Drug Abuse Services
505 Deaderick Street
James K. Polk Building,
Fourth Floor
Nashville, TN 37219
(615) 741-1921

TEXAS
Commission on Alcoholism
809 Sam Houston State Office
Building
Austin, TX 78701
(512) 475-2577
Department of Community Affairs
Drug Abuse Prevention Division
2015 South Interstate Highway 35
P.O. Box 13166
Austin, TX 78711
(512) 443-4100

UTAH
Department of Social Services
Division of Alcoholism and Drugs
150 West North Temple
Suite 350
P.O. Box 2500
Salt Lake City, UT 84110
(801) 533-6532

VERMONT
Agency of Human Services
Department of Social and
Rehabilitation Services
Alcohol and Drug Abuse Division
103 South Main Street
Waterbury, VT 05676
(802) 241-2170

VIRGINIA
Department of Mental Health and
   Mental Retardation
Division of Substance Abuse
109 Governor Street
P.O. Box 1797
Richmond, VA 23214
(804) 786-5313

WASHINGTON
Department of Social and Health
   Service
Bureau of Alcohol and Substance
   Abuse
Office Building—44 W
Olympia, WA 98504
(206) 753-5866

WEST VIRGINIA
Department of Health
Office of Behavioral Health Services
Division on Alcoholism and Drug
   Abuse
1800 Washington Street East
Building 3 Room 451
Charleston, WV 25305
(304) 348-2276

WISCONSIN
Department of Health and Social
   Services
Division of Community Services
Bureau of Community Programs
Alcohol and Other Drug Abuse
   Program Office
1 West Wilson Street
P.O. Box 7851
Madison, WI 53707
(608) 266-2717

WYOMING
Alcohol and Drug Abuse Programs
Hathaway Building
Cheyenne, WY 82002
(307) 777-7115, Ext. 7118

GUAM
Mental Health & Substance Abuse
   Agency
P.O. Box 20999
Guam 96921

PUERTO RICO
Department of Addiction Control
   Services
Alcohol Abuse Programs
P.O. Box B-Y Rio Piedras Station
Rio Piedras, PR 00928
(809) 763-5014

Department of Addiction Control
   Services
Drug Abuse Programs
P.O. Box B-Y Rio Piedras Station
Rio Piedras, PR 00928
(809) 764-8140

VIRGIN ISLANDS
Division of Mental Health,
   Alcoholism & Drug Dependency
   Services
P.O. Box 7329
Saint Thomas, Virgin Islands 00801
(809) 774-7265

AMERICAN SAMOA
LBJ Tropical Medical Center
Department of Mental Health Clinic
Pago Pago, American Samoa 96799

TRUST TERRITORIES
Director of Health Services
Office of the High Commissioner
Saipan, Trust Territories 96950

Further Reading

Bakalar, James B., and Lester Grinspoon. *Drug Control in a Free Society*. Cambridge: Cambridge University Press, 1984.

Brecher, Edward M., and the editors of *Consumer Reports*. *Licit and Illicit Drugs: The Consumers Union Report on Narcotics, Stimulants, Depressants, Inhalants, Hallucinogens, and Marijuana — Including Caffeine, Nicotine and Alcohol*. Boston: Little, Brown, 1972.

Burnham, J. C. "New Perspectives on the Prohibition 'Experiment' of the 1920s." *Journal of Social History* 2 (1968): 51–68.

Drug Abuse Council. *The Facts About 'Drug Abuse'*. New York: Macmillan, 1980.

Institute of Medicine, National Academy of Sciences. *Marijuana and Health: Report of Study*. Washington, D.C.: National Academy Press, 1982.

Jaffe, Jerome H. "Drug Addiction and Drug Abuse." In *The Pharmacological Basis of Therapeutics*, edited by A. G. Gilman, L. S. Goodman, and A. Gilman, 7th ed. New York: Macmillan, 1985.

Kanner, Ronald M., and Kathleen M. Foley. "Patterns of Narcotic Drug Use in a Cancer Pain Clinic." *Annals of the New York Academy of Sciences* 362:161.

Moore, Mark, and Dean Gerstein, eds. *Alcohol and Public Policy: Beyond the Shadow of Prohibition*. Washington, D.C.: National Academy Press, 1981.

Musto, David. *The American Disease: Origins of Narcotic Control*. New Haven: Yale University Press, 1973.

National Commission on Marijuana and Drug Abuse. Second Report, and appendices. *Drug Use in America: Problem in Perspective*. Washington, D.C.: U.S. Government Printing Office, 1973.

National Narcotics Intelligence Consumers Committee. *Narcotics Intelligence Estimate: Drug Enforcement Administration, Washington, D. C., 1984*.

Glossary

addiction a condition caused by repeated drug use, characterized by a compulsive urge to continue using the drug, a tendency to increase the dosage, and a physiological and/or psychological dependence

association a weak link between an action and a result, as in "an association between smoking and cancer." Evidence based on association is not as strong as causal evidence, which is taken as proof of a thesis

black market the underground market in which illegal goods are bought and sold

cannabinoids the 421 chemical compounds identified to date in the marijuana plant

chronic marked by long duration or frequent recurrence

compulsive describing repeated, irrational behavior characterized by lack of self-control

DEA Drug Enforcement Administration, a branch of the Department of Justice and the chief police authority on drug matters

decriminalization a policy of lightening criminal penalties for drug possession, but not making a drug legal

experimental therapy special medical treatment in which new methods are used, often at a university clinic or research center

FDA Food and Drug Administration, the federal agency that controls prescription and over-the-counter drugs

hallucinogen a drug that produces sensory impressions that have no basis in reality

immune system a complex array of cells, organs, and functions in the body that protects it against invasion by toxins, foreign material, and disease

maintenance therapy providing addicts with a legal source of drugs on which they depend, to help them control their habit

NIDA National Institute on Drug Abuse, a research funding and review organization in the Department of Health and Human Services

NORML National Organization for the Reform of the Marijuana Laws, a Washington, D.C., group that campaigns for the legalization of marijuana

opiate any compound derived from the milky juice of the poppy plant *Papaver somniferum*, including opium, morphine, codeine, and heroin

overdose a large quantity of a drug, taken accidentally or on purpose, that causes temporary or permanent damage to the body and may be fatal

physical dependence an adaption of the body to the presence of a drug such that its absence produces withdrawal symptoms

psychoactive altering mood and/or behavior

psychological dependence a condition in which the drug user craves a drug to maintain a sense of well-being and feels discomfort when deprived of it

Schedule I, II, etc. categories under the Controlled Substances Act, under which drugs are ranked by their threat to society and value to medicine. Schedule I drugs are considered to have no medical value and pose the greatest threat

THC tetrahydrocannabinol, the chief psychoactive chemical in marijuana

tolerance a decrease of susceptibility to the effects of a drug due to its continued administration, resulting in the user's need to increase the drug dosage in order to achieve the effects experienced previously

withdrawal the physiological and psychological effects of discontinued use of a drug after a long period of use. In heroin addicts, the period of withdrawal lasts 7 to 10 days.

PICTURE CREDITS

Index

Eliot Marshall is a senior writer for *Science* magazine, the weekly publication of the American Association for the Advancement of Science. He has been employed on the News and Comment staff for eight years reporting on environmental health, nuclear energy, and science policy. He has also served as a senior editor at *The New Republic*.

Solomon H. Snyder, M.D., is Distinguished Service Professor of Neuroscience, Pharmacology and Psychiatry at The Johns Hopkins University School of Medicine. He has served as president of the Society for Neuroscience and in 1978 received the Albert Lasker Award in Medical Research. He has authored *Uses of Marijuana, Madness and the Brain, The Troubled Mind, Biological Aspects of Mental Disorder,* and edited *Perspective in Neuropharmacology: A Tribute to Julius Axelrod.* Professor Snyder was a research associate with Dr. Axelrod at the National Institutes of Health.

Barry L. Jacobs, Ph.D., is currently a professor in the program of neuroscience at Princeton University. Professor Jacobs is author of *Serotonin Neurotransmission and Behavior* and *Hallucinogens: Neurochemical, Behavioral and Clinical Perspectives.* He has written many journal articles in the field of neuroscience and contributed numerous chapters to books on behavior and brain science. He has been a member of several panels of the National Institute of Mental Health.

Joann Ellison Rodgers, M.S. (Columbia), became Deputy Director of Public Affairs and Director of Media Relations for the Johns Hopkins Medical Institutions in Baltimore, Maryland, in 1984 after 18 years as an award-winning science journalist and widely read columnist for the Hearst newspapers.